SO-AXR-416

THE
MAN
WHO GOT
CAPONE

For
JUDITH WILSON

who one morning left open the front door of her home at
2910 Tennyson Street in Washington and was kind
enough to invite me in; and who, while standing at her
dining room table making a lime and sour cream gela-
tin mold, proceeded to tell me all about her husband
Frank—the man who got Capone.

THE MAN WHO GOT CAPONE

by

FRANK SPIERING

The Bobbs-Merrill Company, Inc.
Indianapolis/New York

Copyright © 1976 by Frank Spiering

All rights reserved, including the right of reproduction
in whole or in part in any form
Published by the Bobbs-Merrill Company, Inc.
Indianapolis   New York

Designed by Helen Rudzinski
Manufactured in the United States of America

Second Printing

Library of Congress Cataloging in Publication Data

Spiering, Frank.
  The man who got Capone.

  Includes index.
  1. Capone, Alphonse, 1899–1947. 2. Wilson,
Frank John, 1888–1970.   3. United States.
Office of Internal Revenue.   I. Title.
HV6248.C17S64   364.1′092′4 [B]   76-11626
ISBN 0-672-52231-4

CONTENTS

Contents

PREFACE

What is a hero? Is he a mythical pop figure—a Wyatt Earp, a Pat Garrett, a "Doc" Holliday? (I purposely avoid reference to any in the twentieth century, as there are so few candidates. In addition, the achievements of those who come to mind seem unavoidably controversial. It is disturbing that we seem to have replaced them with the John Wayne type, the Bogart hero.) On one hand, we live in a time of extreme self-criticism, primarily because so many of the things we have been taught we should revere now seem utterly ignoble. On the other, our present attitudes tend to be so artificial that a genuine hero is often overlooked. Instead, we seem to adulate those who facilely assume heroic guises.

Ironically, we have never more needed a real-life illustrative figure who embodies strength of character, integrity, selflessness and unfaltering courage. Our age seems dominated by a terrific polarization of human attitudes toward money and power. It would appear that there is no longer any basis for law and order; the god of the moment is money, legally or illegally obtained. We submit our political leaders to the closest scrutiny, yet we allow crime to flourish in the streets. We have been lured into sympathizing with the Mafia godfather; once an inscrutable, unseen figure at the head of a decidedly corrupt empire, he is now the successful businessman living next door who loves his wife, goes bowling, plays with his kids, etc.

This is the story of a real hero, a man of fanatical persistence and unshakable integrity. It is only fitting that he should have been pitted against our country's most genuine villain.

Frank Wilson never set out to get Capone. He had none of the egotism of certain crime fighters operating in the twenties and thirties who specialized in "crime busts" and "daring captures" of wanted criminals. Obviously, this was why he never became famous.

His full activity was given over to documents, details, and testimony which he painstakingly prepared to be used in a court of law to ensure that justice prevail in the midst of what appeared to be absolute corruption.

This is a true story. Frank Wilson really lived. He never carried a gun.* He armed himself instead with facts.

---

* He once remarked that he was so nearsighted that he probably would not have been able to hit anything with one anyway.

PART I

"Ninety percent of the people of Cook County drink and gamble, and my offense has been to furnish them with those amusements. Whatever else they may say, my booze has been good, and my games have been on the square. Public service is my motto."

—Al Capone

1
McSWIGGIN

William H. McSwiggin was the smartest, toughest prosecutor on Robert Emmett Crowe's staff. Because of the unparalleled number of capital sentences he had obtained, he was referred to by the press as "the Hanging Prosecutor." Whether gathering evidence against criminals or pounding away at them in court, he was merciless. In 1924 alone, he won convictions in nine capital cases.

William H. McSwiggin was twenty-six years old. This dapper young Irishman with the coal-black hair and blue eyes was State's Attorney Crowe's pride. Having graduated with high honors from DePaul University, McSwiggin earned his way through law school working day and night as a movie theater usher, dance hall bouncer, department store salesman, trucker, and special agent for the Railway Express Agency. His academic distinction, and the fact that he had campaigned vigorously for Crowe's reelection in 1920, brought him to the state's attorney's attention. Crowe offered him a job as his assistant.

The Man Who Got Capone

McSwiggin was a bachelor, the only son among the five children of Sergeant Anthony McSwiggin of the Chicago Police Force. He lived with his parents and four sisters at 4946 West Washington Boulevard. He had grown up on Chicago's West Side, in a rough Irish neighborhood, where he was a comrade of such future gangsters as William and Edward "Spike" O'Donnell, Jim Doherty and Tom "Red" Duffy.

McSwiggin's father continually urged him to break off with the disreputable companions of his youth, but he wouldn't listen. His friends were an ongoing source of information; they knew where witnesses could be uncovered—names, places. In return, Bill would help them when he could. It seemed more than a coincidence that in October 1924 he failed as prosecutor to convict his boyhood chum, Jim Doherty, for the murder of Eddie Tancl.

By 1925, Chicago was a battlefield. Since 1920, when Prohibition had gone into effect, profits from bootlegging had dwarfed those of every other underworld activity. Chicago's bootlegging activities were presided over by Johnny Torrio, whose uncle, Chicago gangster Big Jim Colosimo, had originally hired him to liquidate members of the Black Hand, a Sicilian organization that was pressuring his operation.

From the moment he arrived in Chicago, Torrio had realized that his uncle's days were numbered. Colosimo's old-fashioned methods could never keep pace with the mushrooming underworld activity resulting from the passage of the Volstead Act. He soon decided that the time had come to make a move on his own. But he needed a tough, merciless lieutenant to lead his shock troops.

From New York, Torrio summoned a protégé of his,

[4]

a bullet-headed twenty-three-year-old roughneck, and offered him a generous income and half the profits of the bootleg trade if he would come to Chicago to handle the competition. Al Capone accepted.

Al Capone was born and grew up under the shadow of the Williamsburg Bridge in the Greenpoint section of Brooklyn. Gabriel Capone, a barber of Neapolitan origin, and his wife Teresa baptized their son Alphonse at St. Michael's Church on the corner of Tillary and Lawrence streets while hordes of ragged children played stickball outside on the street.

Alphonse Capone's schooling began at P.S. 7 on Adams Street. His teacher later remembered him as "a swarthy, sullen, troublesome boy." He was big and strong for his age, quick-tempered, and murderous when angered. In winter his nose tended to run, a weakness for which his schoolmates ridiculed him. His classmates called him "Macaroni."

Alphonse began second grade at P.S. 113 on Butler Street. Up to the sixth grade he maintained a B average. Then, mainly because of truancy, he fell behind in arithmetic and grammar. His attendance kept dropping. When a teacher reproved him, his volcanic temper erupted, and he struck her in the face. Beaten by the principal, he quit school, never to return.

Al headed for the streets, where he found freedom. But he learned not to roam too far. The easterly stretch of Flushing Avenue near his home was a Sicilian stronghold and was thus unhealthy for Neapolitans. Vicious knife fighters, the Sicilian gangs had adapted to Brooklyn street combat the ancient practice of disfiguring an enemy: they would slit his face from ear to ear.

Street gangs flourished in every section of New

[5]

York. Al was soon "adopted" by Johnny Torrio, already a well-known underworld figure. Torrio enormously influenced his young protégé. "I looked on Johnny like my adviser and father," Capone admitted years later. It was Torrio's influence that led Al to join the Five Pointers. The toughest gang in the city, the Five Pointers specialized in knifings, bludgeonings and shootings. They controlled Manhattan's Lower East Side, from Fourteenth Street to City Hall and from the Bowery to Broadway, almost directly across the Williamsburg Bridge from Al's home. The Lower East Side of Manhattan had undergone little change since Charles Dickens, in his *American Notes,* described "these narrow ways . . . reeking everywhere with dirt and filth . . . hideous tenements which take their name from robbery and murder."

The Five Pointers enjoyed the protection of various political bosses. In return, during elections, the gang's members could be counted on to intimidate, slug, kidnap, or steal ballots, even though most of them had not even reached voting age. Al distinguished himself from the first.

As Al grew into his teens, Frank Yale, the national head of the Unione Siciliane, heard about him. He hired him to work as a bouncer and bartender at his nightclub, the Harvard Inn. Al's huge fists could strike with the impact of a pile driver. He was also fast and accurate with a gun, having perfected his marksmanship by shooting at beer bottles in the cellar of Brooklyn's Adonis Social Club, a favorite Italian hangout.

One evening while working at the Harvard Inn, Al made an offensive remark to one of the customers, the sister of Frank Galluccio. Galluccio went for Al's face with a pocket knife. When the wounds healed, an ugly

[6]

four-inch scar remained, cutting across Al's left jaw. In the words of a dossier compiled by federal agents, it was an "oblique scar of 4" across cheek 2" in front left ear—vertical scar 2½" on left jaw—oblique scar 2½" under left ear on neck." Capone later maintained that he was wounded by shrapnel while fighting as a machine gunner in France with the famous "Lost Battalion" of the Seventy-seventh Division. But in fact he got no closer to the war than his draft board.

When Johnny Torrio summoned him to Chicago, Capone was already suspected of two murders in New York and was facing indictment for a third. He lost no time in leaving for Chicago.

On May 11, 1920, five months after the Volstead Act went into effect, Big Jim Colosimo was shot to death by an unknown assassin in the vestibule of his glittering café on South Wabash Avenue. Torrio and his new lieutenant, Al Capone, took over.

In the next few years the situation became so violent that even Torrio was edged into the background. Early in 1925, after being maimed and almost murdered, he was finally forced to leave Chicago, passing on his entire interest in the breweries and distilleries to Capone.

Capone's personality was far different from Torrio's. While Torrio was quiet-spoken, trying constantly to maintain an air of respectability, Capone had developed into a vicious killer.

At Torrio's departure, Capone took stock of the struggle that lay before him. In order to survive, he would have to subjugate or destroy every other major gang in the city of Chicago. His bitterest foes were William H. McSwiggin's friends, the O'Donnells, "Red" Duffy and Jim Doherty. They had begun pushing beer in

Cicero. Capone had threatened all-out war if their activities continued, but each day the Irishmen grew bolder in their encroachments.

Cicero was a suburb adjoining Chicago on the west, with a population of 60,000. The town was incorporated in 1867, and a charter was granted in 1869. In the twenties Cicero had a larger percentage of private home ownership than any other community of its size in the world. Its inhabitants were principally first- and second-generation Americans from Central Europe. The majority were Bohemians who could not comprehend a law that denied them a glass or two of beer after a hard day's work. Thus, they readily broke the Eighteenth Amendment. The neighborhood saloon with its familiar swinging doors and brass footrails and spittoons went right on serving beer during Prohibition, while politicians closed their eyes, in return for steady graft and protection money.

In the midst of this atmosphere of petty lawlessness, Al "Scarface" Capone planned to establish an empire.

Most of the Cicero beer drinkers were family men who had no desire for the companionship of strange young women or even for gambling. When Capone opened up establishments for such purposes in their home town, they were stunned. But Capone's customers started coming from Chicago. As time went on, Ciceronians were shocked and saddened as the name of their town became synonymous with crime, gang wars and cold-blooded murder.

Capone chose as his official headquarters a centrally located two-story building on Twenty-second Street known as the Hawthorne Inn. Bulletproof steel shutters were affixed to every window. At each entrance an armed lookout was stationed. Four plaster columns painted green supported the lobby ceiling. On the walls hung stuffed big-game heads. Red-carpeted stairs rose to the second-floor bedrooms, where Capone, his associates and their mistresses spent their days and nights.

Capone recruited a corps of triggermen that included Phil D'Andrea, a rifleman who could split a quarter in midair; William "Three-Fingered" Jack White, a crack left-handed killer whose right hand had been smashed in boyhood by a brick falling from a building under construction (White, as sensitive about his disfigurement as Capone was about his facial scars, constantly wore gloves in public, the empty fingers stuffed with cotton); Sam "Golf Bag" Hunt, who used a shotgun concealed in a golf bag (Hunt explained to a detective who once opened the bag, "I'm going to shoot some pheasants." His first shotgun victim failed to die and was known in gangland thereafter as "Hunt's hole in one"); and the young man Capone valued above the others, "Machine Gun" Jack McGurn, who was an avid collector of women, preferably blondes, and who parted his black hair in the middle and slicked it down with pomade until it lay as flat and sleek as Rudolph Valentino's. (McGurn was responsible for at least twenty-two killings. His famed gesture, after chopping down a victim, was to press a nickel into the corpse's hand.)

By April 1925 the Chicago scene was ready to burst wide open. Capone and his Irish competition were poised to lunge at each other's throats. Harry Madigan, the proprietor of the Pony Inn, a Cicero saloon located at 5613 West Roosevelt Road, related:

Capone came to me and said I would have to buy his beer, so I did. . . . Doherty and O'Donnell came to me and said they could sell me better beer than Capone beer, which was then

[9]

needled. They did, and it cost fifty dollars a barrel, where Capone charged me sixty. I changed, and upon my recommendation so did several other Cicero saloonkeepers.

On April 27, 1925, at 6:00 P.M., Bill McSwiggin was at his parents' home eating his supper when Red Duffy drove by. Leaving his meal unfinished, McSwiggin followed Duffy out to the street, remarking to his father that he was going to play cards in nearby Berwyn. McSwiggin and Red Duffy then got into Jim Doherty's car. In the back seat were William and Myles O'Donnell. The five men took off down the street.

They had gone only a few blocks when the car's engine began to sputter. Pulling into a West Side garage, Doherty left the car for repairs. The five men switched to William O'Donnell's new Lincoln sedan. A sixth man, former police officer Edward Hanley, joined them. Hanley ended up driving.

Instead of heading for Berwyn, they began roaming through Cicero, drinking beer in various saloons, laughing, telling stories and carrying on. After two hours, they arrived at Harry Madigan's Pony Inn. They were now exactly one mile north of Capone's headquarters at the Hawthorne Inn.

At 8:15 one of Capone's henchmen recognized O'Donnell's Lincoln sedan and spotted the six men inside the Pony Inn. He hurried to the Hawthorne Inn to tell Capone.

Upon hearing the news, Capone tore from behind a sliding panel a Thompson submachine gun and an extra 100-cartridge magazine. Assembling his triggermen, he instructed them to fetch five cars:

A lead car to ram any police flivvers the motorcade might encounter during the getaway;

McSwiggin

Two cars to move close behind the lead car, but hugging the curb so that they could block traffic at the street intersections until the car carrying Capone and three other armed men got past;

Capone's driver to keep fifty feet behind the first three cars;

The fifth car to cover the rear and, in case of pursuit, to stage an accident, paralyzing traffic.

Within fifteen minutes Capone and his men were lined up half a block from the Pony Inn.

At 8:30 Bill McSwiggin and his friends, sodden with beer, emerged.

As the six men crossed the sidewalk toward the Lincoln, Capone's motorcade bore down on them, machine guns blazing.

A Mrs. Bach who lived above the saloon remembered seeing the machine guns "spitting fire" from the passing cars.

Duffy, Doherty and Bill McSwiggin were almost sawed in half by the blasts. But Hanley and William and Myles O'Donnell saved themselves by diving headlong to the pavement beside the sedan. The O'Donnells panicked. With the prospect of having to face awkward questions if they took their wounded companions to a hospital, they decided to take them to William's house on nearby Parkside Avenue and call a doctor. Bill McSwiggin, with at least twenty slugs in his back and neck, twisted in agony on the sidewalk. Both of Doherty's legs had been shattered and his chest ripped open. The O'Donnells bundled them into the sedan. Red Duffy, who appeared beyond help, was left propped up against a tree.

Before they reached the O'Donnell house, McSwiggin and Doherty died. Leaving Doherty in the car, the

[11]

O'Donnells carried McSwiggin into the house. They emptied his pockets, cut all identifying marks from his clothing and carried him back to the car. Driving cautiously away from the city, the O'Donnells halted beside a lonely stretch of prairie and dumped McSwiggin's body.

At ten o'clock that evening a motorist chanced upon the body on the deserted outskirts of Berwyn. The police delivered it to the city morgue. It was midnight before a Chicago newspaper reporter identified it as that of State's Attorney Crowe's young prosecutor.

The morning headlines erupted with the violent news. Chicagoans had come to view with complacency the gang wars that had claimed more than two hundred lives in four years. "They only kill each other," ran the stereotype. But the murder of an assistant state's attorney startled the country.

State's Attorney Crowe's office was besieged with inquiries. Why was his prize assistant driving around Cicero with four notorious hoodlums? What had he been doing drinking bootleg beer with them, when only a few months before he had tried so hard (or so it seemed) to send one of them to the gallows?

Realizing that his political career was at stake, Crowe responded with a fiery proclamation: "It will be a war to the hilt against these gangsters." He ordered 100 city detectives deputized and sent into the suburbs to raid saloons, speakeasies, gambling houses and brothels. Every known hoodlum was to be arrested on sight. Crowe himself headed the Cicero raiding party, offering from his own pocket a reward of $5,000 for information leading to the arrest of McSwiggin's murderers.

The first place Crowe raided was the Hawthorne Inn. The ledgers and business records found there were taken to the state's attorney's office—where they remained, unexamined.

But the fix was in. Even though Crowe and his raiders made a tremendous commotion, a week after McSwiggin's murder the Chicago *Tribune* reported:

The police have no more actual evidence as to the motives of the shooting and the identity of the killer than they did when it happened.

On the day the *Tribune* ran its story, Crowe issued the following statement to reporters:

It has been established to the satisfaction of the state's attorney's office and the detective bureau that Capone in person led the slayers of McSwiggin.

The dead man's father, Police Sergeant Anthony McSwiggin, told reporters, "I thought my life was over, but it's only begun. I'll never rest until I've killed my boy's slayers or seen them hanged. That's all I have to live for now."

When Capone was asked whether he killed McSwiggin, he replied, "Of course I didn't kill him. Why should I? I liked the kid. Only the day before, he was up to my place, and when he went home I gave him a bottle of scotch for his old man."

Three days before that interview, however, Capone had fled Chicago, terrified that the police might shoot him on sight. When he returned two months later, he announced: "I'm no squawker, but I'll tell what I know about this case. All I ask is a chance to prove that I had nothing to do with the killing of my friend Bill McSwiggin . . . he was a fine young fellow."

[13]

Regarding the O'Donnells and the allegation that the shooting was in retaliation for their attempts to push beer in his territory, Capone scoffed, "I wasn't in the beer racket and didn't care where they sold. Just a few days before that shooting, my brother Ralph and the O'Donnells were at a party together."

Capone was charged with murder and ordered to appear before Federal Court Justice Thomas Lynch. He was represented by his attorney, Thomas Nash, of the law firm of Ahern and Nash.

Within minutes, Assistant State's Attorney George E. Gorman had withdrawn the murder charge. "This complaint," he admitted, "was made . . . on cursory information. Subsequent investigation could not legally substantiate the information." Justice Lynch thereupon dismissed the case.

As Capone sauntered out of the courtroom, beaming, Sergeant Anthony McSwiggin sobbed to a reporter, "They pinned a medal on him and turned him loose." The old man never recovered from his bitterness. He was often heard to murmur, "They killed me, too, when they killed my boy."

Four successive grand juries failed to secure an indictment. Finally, when the fifth grand jury was being formed, Judge Charles A. McDonald persuasively stepped forward. " I know who killed McSwiggin," he stated.

Two new clues and two new witnesses had been found. He went on, "[But] it is necessary to keep the names of the witnesses secret. The moment any of the witnesses learn that they are wanted, they disappear, or are even killed." The grand jury adjourned the first day, pending the presentation of the promised evidence. No new clues or new witnesses ever materialized.

[14]

McSwiggin

A sixth special grand jury brought the investigation to a fumbling conclusion in October 1925, six months after McSwiggin's murder. The Illinois Crime Survey reflected:

. . . the McSwiggin case marks the beginning of intense public interest in organized crime. . . . The very failure of the grand juries in solving the mystery of McSwiggin's death has raised many puzzling and disturbing questions in the minds of intelligent citizens about the reasons for the breakdown of constituted government in Chicago and Cook County.

2
CHICAGO SURRENDERS

Big Bill Thompson was the epitome of the corrupt politician. "I'm wetter than the middle of the Atlantic Ocean," he boasted.

Al Capone took him at his word.

In 1926, when Thompson was running for mayor of Chicago, Capone contributed $260,000 to his campaign fund. He applied every known technique of bribery and terrorism in Thompson's behalf. Capone soon became credited with the slogan, "Vote early and vote often."

Strangely, Big Bill Thompson's major campaign plank had nothing to do with Prohibition. In a move to divert attention from the cry of many Chicagoans, "Who killed McSwiggin?" and from their accusations that he was in collusion with Capone, Thompson launched an assault on the history books in Chicago's public schools, charging that they were partial to the British. Promising, if elected, to fire school superintendent William McAndrew, he claimed that the ideals Americans had been taught to revere "are subtly sneered at in these books . . . so that your children may blush with shame when studying the history of their country." He maintained that the books contained facts "that are distorted . . . to glorify England and vilify America." Hugging an American flag to his breast, he ranted, "This is the issue! What was good enough for George Washington is good enough for Bill Thompson. . . . America First! The American who says 'America second' speaks the tongue of Benedict Arnold and Aaron Burr. . . . There never was an Englishman who was the equal of an American, and if there was, he could make a million dollars in an hour and a half by beating that brave Gene Tunney, our world champion fighter."

The focus of his attack was the king of England, whom he threatened to personally kick "in the seat of the pants" if he should ever set foot in Chicago. "This King George! If King George had his way, there'd be a million American boys in China today to fight the battle for the dirty Englishmen and help the king make a billion dollars in the opium trade."

To question why this line of reasoning did not sting the intelligence of the average Chicagoan is to overlook the existent climate of thought epitomized by novelist Sinclair Lewis's character George F. Babbitt:

He serenely believed that the one purpose of the real estate business was to make money for George F. Babbitt. True, it was a good advertisement at Boosters' Club lunches, and all the varieties of Annual Banquets to which Good Fellows were invited, to speak sonorously of Unselfish Public Service, the Broker's Obligation to Keep Inviolate the Trust of His Clients, and a thing called Ethics, whose nature was confusing but if you had it you were a High-class Realtor and if you hadn't you were a shyster, a piker, and a fly-by-night. . . .

Babbitt spoke well—and often—at these orgies of commercial righteousness about the "realtor's functions as a seer

[18]

of the future development of the community, and as a prophetic engineer clearing the pathway for inevitable changes"—which meant that a real estate broker could make money by guessing which way the town would grow. This guessing he called Vision. . . .

He did not know whether the police force was too large or too small, or whether it was in alliance with gambling and prostitution. He knew the means of fireproofing, but he did not know how many firemen there were in the city, how they were trained and paid, or how complete their apparatus. He sang eloquently the advantages of proximity of school buildings to rentable homes, but he did not know—he did not know that it was worthwhile to know—whether the city schoolrooms were properly heated, lighted, ventilated, furnished.

Chicago's Babbitts lined up behind Big Bill Thompson, a towering ex-athlete with a snaggled front tooth. Thompson was always pictured wearing a gigantic fur coat. He longed for the life of the cowboy, and the only reading he did was dime thrillers about the Wild West. He had a natural gift for campaign-tent oratory and knew instinctively how to arouse the prejudices of ethnic and national groups. He prodded the Negroes, "If you want to shoot craps, go ahead and do it." He fanned the prejudices of Chicago's Irish and Italian voters by calling the British "seedy and untrustworthy." He promised the socially conscious do-gooders of the silk-stocking wards: "I'll clean up this city and drive out the crooks!" All the while, Al Capone was financing his campaign.

Thompson made peaceful overtures to State's Attorney Crowe, who accepted them despite an earlier statement of dedication that "any man interested in protecting gambling and vice I refuse to travel along with, politically or otherwise."

[19]

Reacting to opponent John Dill Robertson's cry of "Who killed McSwiggin?" Thompson irrelevantly retorted, "Imagine anyone thinking of electing a man for mayor with a name like John Dill Pickle Robertson!" Further responding to a blast from a second opponent, Ed Litsinger, that he was in collusion with criminals, Thompson thundered angrily, "Ed Litsinger's been making statements about me. I've told you and I'll tell you again that he's the biggest liar that ever was a candidate for mayor. And you know what else? He plays handball in the semi-nude! That's right, with only a little pair of pants on. I know one thing, you won't find Bill Thompson having his picture taken in the semi-nude."

Capone knew he was backing a winner. Thompson would do anything to obtain votes. He not only swore to open up the brothels, the saloons and the gambling casinos that the former administration had shut down; he now vowed to open 10,000 new ones.

On April 5, election day, Capone's Hotel Metropole suite was a veritable annex to the Thompson campaign headquarters on the sixteenth floor of the Hotel Sherman. Capone, cigar in mouth, sat hunched over a mahogany conference table behind a battery of nine telephones, issuing commands to his forces scattered throughout the city, to triggermen, sluggers, kidnappers, bombers. . . .

Later that evening, in the Hotel Sherman's Louis XIV Ballroom, Thompson, his breath reeking of bourbon, leaped up on a chair, brandished a ten-gallon hat and bellowed, "The lead is now 52,000! I thank you one and all, I thank you. Tell 'em, cowboys, tell 'em! I told you I'd ride 'em high and wide!"

Thompson's triumphant entry into Chicago's City

Hall heralded an unparalleled era of bloodshed, racketeering and civic corruption.

Within a month of the election, Capone had enlarged his Hotel Metropole headquarters to fifty rooms, reserving the Hawthorne Inn as a secondary base of operations. From City Hall and the Police Department came a flood of purchasable magistrates, administrators, politicians. Capone's killers were furnished with officially stamped cards reading: "To the Police Department—you will extend the courtesies of this department to the bearer." Capone's ace triggerman Phil D'Andrea wore the star of a municipal court bailiff and drew a salary of $200 a month from the city. The police were ordered either to ignore the murders committed by Capone's henchmen or to enter them in the records as "unsolved." Capone estimated the total payoff to police at this time at $30,000,000 a year.

The Metropole teemed with police officers, politicians and gangsters. A bar for free drinks was set up in the hotel lobby. Capone and his lieutenants had their own upper-story service bars. In the basement was kept a private stock of wines and liquors valued at $100,000. Accessible women freely roamed the hotel; nearly every top Caponeite had a favorite mistress whom he set up in one of the suites. Several rooms were provided for gambling.

Capone's plan to keep everyone in line met few obstacles. When Boss Morris Eller, Thompson's choice for Republican committeeman of the Twentieth Ward, ran for election, his candidacy was challenged by a Negro attorney, Octavius Granady. Never before had a Negro demanded political equality in the Twentieth Ward. On the night of the election, Granady was standing outside the polls, chatting with supporters, when a shot from a passing car barely missed him. Granady jumped into his car and fled. The assassin's car turned and followed, shotguns blazing. Granady's car crashed into a tree. An easy target in the headlights of his pursuers, the black attorney was torn apart by a volley of slugs.

Eventually, four policemen and three gangsters stood trial for the murder. All seven were acquitted.

Capone found that he could run things as easily from his estate in Miami as he could from Chicago. Seated by his pool, he calmly directed the killings of rivals and political foes. A ten-foot wall of concrete surrounded his estate. Heavy oaken portals behind the spiked iron entrance gate completely shut off any view of the interior. A house phone beside the gate enabled callers to announce themselves. No one was admitted until an armed bodyguard, from his station behind the portals, inspected him. The house where Capone lived, a two-story neo-Spanish structure of white stucco with a flat green-tile roof, was shaded by twelve royal palm trees. Between the house and Miami Bay was Capone's private sixty-by-forty-foot swimming pool, the largest in the area, with one of the first filter systems adaptable to both fresh and salt water. The pool area was bordered on one side by a two-story bathhouse in the style of a Venetian loggia. For fishing and cruising, Capone maintained a variety of vessels, among them a speedboat and a thirty-two-foot cabin cruiser. When his cronies visited him, he liked to take off with a picnic basket of salami sandwiches and beer in a chartered seaplane (at $60 an hour, plus $100 an hour for the pilot) and fly down to Bimini.

Chicago Surrenders

The living room of the Capone mansion was crowded with massive upholstered furniture. A life-size oil painting of Capone and his twelve-year-old son stared down from one wall. The master bedroom at the rear of the main house had a sweeping view of pool, loggia and bay. Capone slept, ate and made love in an immense four-poster, at the foot of which stood a wooden chest full of cash. Capone liked the feel of hard needle spray everywhere on his body, so he had a stall shower built with seven extra shower heads jutting from the sides. The cost of these few extra improvements came close to $100,000.

At this point, Capone grew even more greedy. He wanted to expand his bootleg activities to a nationwide operation. He obtained liquor of the highest quality, had it landed at lake and coastal points by rumrunners from Canada, Cuba and the Bahamas, and began marketing it all over the Midwest.

Although liquor produced the bulk of his profits, he soon edged into racketeering. Within two years of Big Bill Thompson's election as mayor, the state's attorney's office compiled a list of ninety-one Chicago unions and associations that had fallen prey to racketeer rule. These included the Retail Food and Fruit Dealers, the Master Photo Finishers, the Junk Dealers and Peddlers, the Building Trade Council, the City Hall Clerks, the Steamfitters and Plumbers, the Theater Treasurers and Box Office Men, the Bakers, the Excavating Contractors, the Barbers, the Soda Pop Peddlers, the Garbage Haulers, the Electrical Workers, the Clothing Workers, the Motion Picture Operators, the Painters and Decorators, the Carpet Layers, the Undertakers, and the Coal Teamsters. Of the estimated $105,000,000 Capone's

[23]

syndicate grossed in 1928, about $10,000,000 flowed from these rackets. Capone was one of the most successful businessmen in America.

By collecting exorbitant fees from independent businesses at the point of a gun, Capone forced consumer prices up. He tried to take over the Chicago *Tribune* but was opposed head-on by its publisher, Colonel Robert R. McCormick, who admitted that after throwing Capone out of a publishers' meeting, ". . . I traveled around in an armored car with one or two bodyguards."

By the end of 1928, Capone had forced his way into almost every commercial enterprise in Chicago. His brothels and gambling casinos were open everywhere. His breweries and liquor distributors were running at full volume. Not long after Big Bill Thompson's election, a *Daily News* reporter asked the deputy commissioner of police, William P. Russell, why he allowed policy numbers racketeers to operate openly in his district. "I haven't had any order from downtown to interfere in the policy racket, and until I do get such orders, you can bet I'm going to keep my hands off," Deputy Commissioner Russell replied. "Mayor Thompson was elected on the open town platform. . . . I assume the people knew what they wanted when they voted for him. . . . Personally, I don't propose to get mixed up in any jam that will send me to the sticks."

But what about the average Chicagoan? Since 1924 he had been helplessly absorbed into the network of lawlessness and violence that every day increased around him.

On Easter Sunday a published letter from the leaders of Chicago's clergy—Catholic, Protestant and Jewish—spoke out against Big Bill Thompson's machine: "Ours is a government of bombs and bums. . . . O Lord! May there be an awakening of public spirit and consciousness. Grant that we may be awakened to a sense of public shame."

Thompson's response conveyed his brutal cynicism: "Sure, we have crime here . . . we always will have crime. Chicago is just like any other big city. You can get a man's arm broken for so much, a leg for so much. . . ."

At this point, Big Bill Thompson decided to run for the presidency of the United States. Calvin Coolidge had backed out of the Republican candidacy with the cryptic statement: "I do not choose to run for President in 1928." Thompson saw no reason why his flamboyant oratory and his "America First" apothegm should not carry him right into the White House.

Could he actually bull his way into the leadership of the country, as he had so successfully done in Chicago?

Thompson set out on a cross-country train tour. At each station stop, press agents touted him as the founder of the America First movement and distributed patriotic leaflets and buttons, while a quartet sang, "America First and Last and Always." William Randolph Hearst welcomed him at his California ranch, San Simeon. When Thompson returned to Chicago, State's Attorney Crowe, now a full-fledged Thompsonite, lauded him as "a great American. He has done more for Chicago than anything that has happened in my lifetime."

Even Capone decided it was time to improve his public image. He was tired of being pictured as a hoodlum. He seriously considered retaining Ivy Lee, the public relations counselor who had so successfully created the public image of John D. Rockefeller. "There's a lot of people in Chicago that have got me pegged for one of those bloodthirsty mobsters you read about in storybooks," Capone complained, "the kind that tortures his victim, cuts off their ears, puts out their eyes with a red-hot poker and grins while he's doing it." He wanted no longer to appear as the embodiment of savagery, a ruthless gangland lord. "I could bear it all if it weren't for the hurt it brings to my mother and my family. They hear so much about what a terrible criminal I am. It's getting too much for them, and I'm just sick of it all myself." He upheld Cicero as a model of civic virtue, "the cleanest burg in the U.S.A. There's only one gambling house in the whole town, and not a single so-called vice den."

His own business, he proudly claimed, was a boon to his fellow Chicagoans. "I've been spending the best years of my life as a public benefactor. I've given people the light pleasures, shown them a good time."

Asked what a gangster thought about when he killed another in a gang war, Capone replied: "Well, maybe he thinks that the law of self-defense, the way God looks at it, is a little broader than the lawbooks have it. Maybe it means killing a man in defense of your business—the way you make the money to take care of your wife and child. I think it does. You can't blame me for thinking there's worse fellows in the world than me."

John Scalise and Albert Anselmi were trusted lieutenants in the Capone organization. Scalise, heavy-set, with wavy black hair and darting, shadowy eyes; and Anselmi, a natty dresser, pensive, thin featured, a cold, nervous type, had been hired by Capone in 1924 to exterminate Irish gangleader Dion O'Banion. On November 10 of that year Scalise and Anselmi, carrying out Capone's orders, had entered O'Banion's flower shop at 738 North State Street by the rear entrance. Seconds later, when the two emerged, O'Banion lay sprawled amidst a chaotic jumble of crushed flowers, six bullets having been pumped into his throat, arms, chest and brain.

Now, four years later, Scalise and Anselmi joined with Sicilian gunman Giuseppe "Hop Toad" Giunta in a plot to assassinate Capone.

A reward of $50,000 had been offered by Capone's ancient rivals, the Aiellos. Even though they had been forced out of Chicago years earlier, the Aiellos were still seeking revenge.

The offer had already enticed four free-lance killers—New York's Tony Torchio; Tony Russo and Vincent Spicuzza from St. Louis; and Sam Valente from Cleveland—who arrived in Chicago in the spring of 1927. A few days after their arrival, each was found tommy-gunned to death, a nickel clutched in his hand—the signature of Capone's chief triggerman Jack McGurn.

But Scalise, Anselmi, and Giunta were confident. They knew Capone well. They were his friends.

Unfortunately, they underestimated Capone's network of spies.

On May 7, 1928, shortly after the three had made their deal with the Aiellos, Capone invited them to a banquet at the Hawthorne Inn in Cicero. After they had eaten and drunk to satiation, Capone's aides suddenly surrounded them and tied them to their chairs.

Capone picked up a baseball bat and with slow, cool deliberation personally beat each one to death.

Their corpses were later found piled in the back seat of their own car, which had been abandoned near Hammond, Indiana. When the coroner examined the bodies, he found hardly a bone unbroken, hardly an area of flesh that was not mutilated.

George "Bugs" Moran was another of Capone's relentless foes. As Capone's strength grew, Moran hijacked truckload after truckload of Capone's premium booze. He bombed saloons that were buying Capone's beer. His gang twice attempted to kill Capone's trigger-man Jack McGurn. Two of his men, the Gusenberg brothers, finally caught McGurn in a phone booth and opened up on him with a tommy gun. Major surgery and a long hospital confinement were necessary to save McGurn's life.

Moran then set fire to Capone's race track, the Hawthorne Kennel Club. He constantly taunted Capone, calling him "the Beast" and "the Behemoth." He told a reporter that Capone kept himself going day and night by taking pills. "Me, I don't need an aspirin," Moran boasted.

Finally, Moran's antics grew too much for Capone. Capone made a telephone call from his Miami estate on February 11, 1929. Two days later a hijacker telephoned Moran and offered him a truckload of whiskey from Detroit at the bargain price of $57 a case. Moran told him to deliver it around 10:30 the following morning to a warehouse at 2122 North Clark Street.

Seven members of Moran's gang were waiting in the one-story red-brick building for the truck to arrive. Moran was supposed to meet his men there, but he got started for the warehouse late.

The temperature had fallen to fifteen degrees. A bone-chilling wind was blowing off Lake Michigan. Inside the unheated building a pot of coffee percolated on an electric plate. The men crouched around it with their hats and overcoats on. A naked 200-watt bulb hung down over their heads. Just outside, a German shepherd named Highball was tied by a leash to the axle of a truck.

A long black Cadillac, a police gong on its running board and a gunrack behind the driver, slowly cruised up the block and stopped in front of the warehouse. Moran, arriving at the same moment, had just turned the corner when he spotted the car. He quickly ducked back, certain that there was about to be a raid. Four men, two in police uniforms and the other two in civilian clothes, emerged from the car and started for the warehouse. A fifth man remained behind the Cadillac's wheel. The four disappeared inside.

What followed sounded like the chatter of a pneumatic drill. It lasted for a minute or so. It was followed by two single blasts like an automobile backfiring.

The two men in civilian clothes hurried from the warehouse, their hands in the air, followed by the two policemen with drawn guns. They got into the Cadillac and drove off.

It was then that the German shepherd started to yowl, a sad, mournful cry cutting through the silence. The dog would not stop.

Finally a neighbor went to investigate and discovered the carnage. Some of the corpses were held together only by shreds of flesh and bone. Apparently, machine guns had riddled the heads, chests and stomachs of the seven men; when two of the victims still squirmed after the machine guns had finished, shotgun blasts were discharged point-blank into their faces. Along the wall where the seven had stood, blood splashed down the yellowish bricks. Blood from their bodies continued to streak across the oily surface of the stone floor. Only one man might have described what

[29]

happened: somehow, Frank Gusenberg had survived. He lasted a few hours, but all he would say was, "Nobody shot me. I ain't no copper."

No one was ever convicted of the Saint Valentine's Day killings. But Moran got the message. "Only Capone kills like that," he said. When the comment was repeated to him at a gala party at his Palm Island mansion, Capone laughed. "The only man who kills like that is Bugs Moran," he said.

Capone could still joke, but the slaughter on Clark Street had settled nothing. His intended victim, Bugs Moran, had escaped.

In 1929 a conference was convened at the President Hotel in Atlantic City. It was attended by gangsters from all over America, including Jake Guzik, Frank Nitti and Frank Rio from Capone's own organization; Max "Boo Boo" Hoff, Sam Lazar and Charles Schwartz from Philadelphia; and Frank Costello, Lucky Luciano and Arthur Flegenheimer, alias Dutch Schultz, from New York. Capone immediately took over. "I told them," he disclosed later, "there was business enough to make us all rich, and it was time to stop all the killings and look on our business as other men look on theirs, as something to work at and forget when we go home at night."

Capone divided the country into spheres of influence. A supreme executive committee, headed by Capone's old mentor Johnny Torrio, was established to arbitrate all disputes and to mete out punishment to violators of the agreement. Capone acknowledged, "It wasn't an easy matter for men who had been fighting for years to agree on a peaceful business program. But we finally decided to forget the past and begin all over again. We drew up a written agreement, and each signed on the dotted line."

That meeting marked the formal beginning of organized crime in the United States.

In six short years, Al Capone's criminal genius had grown beyond the boundaries of Cicero, until it now threatened the daily existence of every American. Yet Al Capone considered himself, first and foremost, a methodical businessman. As he remarked, "I give the public what the public wants. I never had to send out high-pressure salesmen. I could never meet the demand."

Ironically, he had failed to perform an act that was even then regarded as essential by every businessman in America: he had not filed a federal income tax return.

3
FEVER

Economic conditions are dependent not on a lack or a surplus of money, but on how a nation views itself.

In the 1920s, farmers were having a terrible time. But farmers were only a small part of the population. It was a businessman's world, and business was booming.

In 1919 there had been 6,771,000 passenger cars in service in the United States; by 1929 there were 23,121,000. There seemed to be more money than ever before to buy electric irons, toasters, cigarettes, telephones, refrigerators, cosmetics, records and radios, and to go to the movies.

Americans went to movies more than once a week to see Clara Bow, Rudolph Valentino and Douglas Fairbanks in their latest film stories about swashbuckling romance or reckless heroes (it was still too early for gangster films). They were starstruck by heroes. They adored them.

On May 20, 1927, Charles Lindbergh left from Curtiss Field on Long Island on a journey that many would consider a miracle. The Atlantic had actually been

[33]

crossed by airplane on five prior occasions, but Lindbergh's feat was to capture the anxious attention and the emotions of Americans like nothing before.

Lindbergh was the first to fly it alone.

Young, old, rich, poor, farmer, stockbroker—all flew with him in the *Spirit of St. Louis.* Reports were received:

"Lindbergh's plane has reached the Irish Coast."

"He is crossing over England."

"He is over the Channel."

"He just landed at Le Bourget! A vast crowd of Frenchmen has enthusiastically mobbed him!"

America went wild. Every record for mass excitement and ballyhoo was smashed. For weeks afterward nothing seemed to matter, either to the newspapers or to their readers, but Lindbergh and his story. The New York *Evening World* called it "the greatest feat of a solitary man in the records of the human race." No one thought it extravagant when President Coolidge sent a United States Navy cruiser to bring the young hero and his plane home from France.

Lindbergh was given the Distinguished Flying Cross and the Congressional Medal of Honor. He was offered two and a half million dollars for a tour of the world by air; a 1,300-foot Lindbergh tower was proposed for the city of Chicago; in New York, "the largest dinner ever tendered to an individual in modern history" was held in his honor, and a staggering number of schools, restaurants, corporations, towns and cities sought to share the glory of his name.

What was the reason behind this extraordinary outpouring of admiration and love—toward one man?

The American people had lived through the depressing aftermath of the war and the scandals of the Harding

Administration; they had seen their early ideals and hopes worn thin by scientific doctrines and psychological theories, their religion undermined, their sentimental notions ridiculed. An abundance of money had given them only temporary satisfaction. Romance was a farce, self-dedication passé. History's heroes were ancient ghosts. Something crucial was missing—something they needed to make their dreams whole. They tried to compensate by discovering someone to instantly admire, look up to, emulate. Charles Lindbergh was their hero. So were Babe Ruth, Jack Dempsey, Bobby Jones.

And so was Al Capone.

Capone had blossomed into a contemporary folk hero. An editorial in a Viennese newspaper, quoted by the Chicago press, called Capone "the real mayor of Chicago" and wondered why the voters did not make him so by law as well as in fact. *Le Journal de Paris* dispatched its celebrated crime expert, Georges London, to Chicago to interview him. After Capone invited him to Florida so that he could proudly show him "my beautiful flowers," London concluded, "And the man of fifty corpses, always smiling, gives me his hand, fine and very white." This in contradistinction to Judge Lyle's appraisal of Capone, "He deserves to die . . . a reptile."

But the citizens of the twenties seemed willing to close their eyes to the elements of Capone's power—the bloody murders, corruption of public officials, and his brutal domination of speakeasies, distilleries, brothels, gambling houses, nightclubs, and horse and dog tracks throughout the nation. The most pronounced mood of the times was rebellion. The Volstead Act was their *bête noire*: it had attempted to stop them from drinking.

Fed by increased amounts of money, the rebellion gained orgiastic proportions. As always in a revolution,

[35]

nightmarish elements surfaced. Recklessness threw open the door to lawlessness; unchecked freedom made moral standards seem hollow. "Do what you will" became both theme and impassioned excuse; the youth of the twenties had broken away from an old-fashioned post-Victorian world into a quest for as much hedonistic rioting as their money could buy.

America was on a get-rich-quick binge. It had illegal liquor to buy, new products to consume. Advertising copywriters did not concern themselves with the merits of their products; rather, they appealed to the buyer's wish to have eyes like his favorite movie star; to look young, desirable; to keep up with the Joneses; to be the center of attention; to be envied, loved. A profound sense of inadequacy beset anyone who couldn't afford such things.

Money alone could make real what the advertising world had dreamed up. One road to easy money was the stock market. Another was organized crime.

In a society that worships money, success and power above everything else, a man with Al Capone's ruthlessness can flourish. By 1929 Capone had amassed a fortune of approximately thirty million dollars. He owned business interests that stretched nationwide. For self-protection, he ordered from General Motors a custom-built Cadillac limousine. Weighing seven tons, it had an armor-plated steel body, a steel-hooded gas tank, bulletproof window glass half an inch thick, and, behind the rear seat, a gun compartment with a movable window, enabling passengers to fire at pursuers.* When he went to the theater, he was attended by a bodyguard of eighteen young men in dinner jackets, with guns slung under

* This car was later used by President Franklin Delano Roosevelt as his official limousine.

[36]

their armpits in approved gangster fashion. When his sister was married, thousands milled around the church; Capone presented the bride with a nine-foot wedding cake. He purchased an estate on Palm Island, just off the coast of Miami, where he entertained a hundred guests at a time. Al Capone was twenty-nine years old.

At the Charleston, Indiana, race track, thousands stood and cheered him when he entered with his bodyguards, waving his clasped hands over his head like a prizefighter entering the ring. During the American Derby at Washington Park, U.S. Attorney George Johnson was astounded to hear the band strike up "It's a Lonesome Old Town When You're Not Around" as Capone, a sunburst in yellow suit and yellow tie, took his seat. Droves of race fans rushed forward, eager to shake his hand.

Capone was the first one to admit that he was making a significant contribution to American life. "Yes. It's bootleg while it's on the trucks, but when your host at the club, in the locker room, or on the Gold Coast hands it to you on a silver platter, it's hospitality. What's Al done, then? Some call it bootlegging. Some call it racketeering. I call it a business. They say I violate the Prohibition law. Who doesn't?"

When Eleanor "Cissy" Patterson, editor of the Washington *Herald*, interviewed him, she found him to be glamorous. "Once I looked *at* his eyes. Ice-gray, ice-cold eyes. You can't any more look *into* the eyes of Capone than you can look into the eyes of a tiger." On parting she wished Capone good luck, "and I mean it sincerely." "It has been said with truth," she concluded, "that women have a special kind of sympathy for gangsters. If you don't understand why, consult Dr. Freud."

[37]

Capone had developed a particular finesse in the management of judges and politicians. By the end of the decade, he had gained complete control of the police and politicians in Chicago, had installed his own mayor in office, and had established his personal headquarters on two floors of the Hotel Lexington.

As President Coolidge had declared, the business of America was business; no one had applied this apothegm more effectively than Chicago's swarthy five-foot ten-and-a-half-inch tall, 255-pound lord of vice. From October 11, 1927, to January 15, 1929, no fewer than 157 bombs were set or exploded in the Chicago district, and none of the perpetrators were ever arrested or brought to trial. In desperation, businessmen turned to Capone for protection. He agreed to protect them—for a price.

Attempts were made to stop him—but they were always met by a fixed jury or cold-blooded retribution. Soon, Capone not only controlled politics throughout the State of Illinois but influenced other state governments as well. In Florida, Chief Justice John P. McGoorty appealed to the grand jury to help him thwart Capone's plans to direct his illicit enterprises from there: "[Capone's] most formidable competitors have been ruthlessly exterminated, and his only apparent obstacle toward undisputed sway is the law. . . . The time has come when the public must choose between the rule of the gangster and the rule of the law." Result: Capone was given free rein to operate without interference in the State of Florida.

Everywhere, responsible citizens were beginning to face the reality that the honest residents of Chicago had long ago learned to live with: that their courts were corrupt, their elected officials bribed, their police under the thumb of the underworld. In alarm, they turned anxiously for help to the executive branch of the federal government.

The first agency to respond was the Prohibition Bureau. It sent Eliot Ness, a twenty-six-year-old University of Chicago graduate, to Chicago with a detail of nine hand-picked men, all under thirty and variously skilled in marksmanship, truck driving and wiretapping, to wreck Al Capone's financial empire. In his book, *The Untouchables*, later wildly melodramatized by the television series of the same name, Ness admitted, "I felt a chill of foreboding for my men as I envisioned the violent reaction we would produce in the criminal octopus hovering over Chicago, its tentacles of terror reaching out all over the nation. We had undertaken what might be a suicidal mission. . . . Capone was a man with an extreme sensitivity to the public taste and great cunning as a corruptionist. Bringing all his skills into play, he was able to get more people to work for him—including gangsters, law enforcement officers, political figures and even judges—than any other criminal in history." Unfortunately, Ness craved personal publicity. He kept the press informed of his battle strategy, and when he and his raiders besieged a Capone brewery, he often took along a cameraman to record the scene. Ness himself was a handsome, dashing figure, but his love of notoriety severely limited his effectiveness. He undoubtedly did cause Capone considerable financial loss. However, he did not, as he later claimed, dry up Chicago, with its 20,000-odd places where one could buy a drink, nor did he destroy Al Capone.

On March 4, 1929, Herbert Hoover was inaugurated President of the United States. In his State of the Union message he focused on the fact that organized crime was increasing at an alarming rate. With great solemnity he warned: "The ugly truth is that the lawbreaker, whoever he may be, is the enemy of society. We can no longer gloss over the unpleasant reality which should be made vital in the consciousness of every citizen, that he who condones or traffics with crime, who is indifferent to it and to the punishment of the criminal, or to the lax performance of official duty, is himself the most effective agency for the breakdown of society."

The executive branch of the government had just been presented with an extremely sophisticated and lethal weapon to wield against the mounting tide of crime in the United States. Manley Sullivan, a bootlegger, had filed no tax return on the grounds that income from illegal sources was not taxable and, moreover, that to declare such income would be self-incriminatory within the spirit of the Fifth Amendment. The Supreme Court had ruled against Sullivan, finding no reason why a business that was unlawful should be exempt from paying taxes "that if lawful it would have to pay." As to self-incrimination, the ruling went on, "It would be an extreme if not extravagant application of the Fifth Amendment to say that it authorized a man to refuse to state the amount of his income because it had been made in crime."

It was an unofficial remark by Hoover, however, that laid the groundwork for the government's campaign against the mountain of vice rising in the Midwest.

Before breakfast one morning shortly after his inauguration, the new President, with Secretary of the Treasury Andrew Mellon, was tossing a medicine ball around on the White House lawn near the magnolia tree Andrew Jackson had planted in memory of his wife. It was a form of exercise Hoover engaged in every morning. "Have you got that fellow Capone yet?" Hoover asked, heaving the medicine ball hard at Mellon's chest. Mellon shook his head no as he grabbed the ball and heaved it back. Hoover caught it, then suddenly let fly full thrust at Mellon. "Remember," he prodded as Mellon leaped for the ball, "I want that man Capone in jail."

4
THE INVESTIGATOR

The office of Elmer L. Irey, on the third floor of 1111 Constitution Avenue, Washington, D.C., was directly across the street from that of his rival, J. Edgar Hoover, on the fifth floor of the Justice Department building. Hoover's office and staff were five times larger than Irey's.

The rivalry between the United States Bureau of Investigation* and Irey's Intelligence Unit had first become evident in 1922. During a congressional hearing, Hoover's predecessor, William J. Burns, when asked about Irey, had jeered, "You mean Irey of the Intelligence Unit? Intelligence, bah! That's a misnomer."

But Irey was above such pettiness. In fact, it was his aloofness that created some very special enemies. Twice someone had reported to Irey's superiors that he had been seen dead drunk. This amused them; they were well aware that Elmer L. Irey was a teetotaler.

Irey's private office was comparable in size to that of a successful lawyer in a midwestern town. A large

* Later renamed the Federal Bureau of Investigation.

[43]

American flag occupied a standard near the center of the room, while the small figure of Lincoln standing in the middle of his desk and the portrait of the Great Emancipator on the wall opposite were clues to Irey's middle name.

In 1920 Elmer Irey had been earning $1,800 a year as a stenographer in the Post Office Department in Lynchburg, Virginia. He was in line for promotion to chief stenographer to the Chief of the Post Office Inspectors, then considered the finest governmental investigational unit in the world, when Joseph Callen, a special assistant to Daniel C. Roper, Commissioner of Internal Revenue, approached him with an offer to head a new governmental agency.

Prior to the enactment of the Sixteenth Amendment to the Constitution on February 25, 1913, the principal income of the federal government had consisted of customs duties and excise or indirect taxes. The Revenue Act of 1913, enacted by Congress on October 3 of that year, imposed a normal tax of 1% on the net incomes of individuals, estates, trusts and corporations. The Revenue Act of 1916 practically doubled the normal rates specified in the 1913 act. When the United States entered the World War on April 6, 1917, income tax rates were again increased, and an excess-profits tax feature was added to the law as provided by the Revenue Act of 1917. This act imposed the highest rates of taxation that had ever been known in the history of the country. The surtax of 1% on incomes of more than $20,000 was now expanded to cover net incomes of $5,000 or more, and the rate was graduated up to a maximum of 63%.

The rising rate had created wide-scale occurrences of collusion between certain taxpayers and dishonest tax collectors. Commissioner Roper wanted to set up an agency to remedy this situation, which was causing the Internal Revenue Bureau a great deal of embarrassment. Callen suggested to Roper: "Maybe we can get some post office inspectors. They can spot a missing penny quicker than anybody in the world." With Commissioner Roper's approval, Callen called his friend Elmer Irey to ask if he was interested in heading the new unit.

Irey later denied that he had been reluctant to accept Callen's offer. "I wanted the job as soon as it was offered. Callen just took a long time getting around to telling me I'd be making $2,500 a year."

Irey was thirty-one when he formed what he called the Special Intelligence Unit of the Treasury. His reason for the word "Special" is vague. However, "Intelligence" was a highly fashionable word at the time, having acquired a certain glamour during the war.

Initially, the new agency, which consisted of Irey, his assistant Harry Woolf, and five special agents, was charged with the duty of investigating attempts to defraud the federal government of taxes. But in a short time, its duties broadened to include investigations directed by the commissioner and the Secretary of the Treasury. In the decade that followed, the new unit gained little public notice. Only occasionally was it mentioned in the press in connection with tax fraud disclosures or prosecutions.

Meanwhile J. Edgar Hoover's Bureau of Investigation, across the street, was being touted as the leading governmental investigative agency. Understandably, then, Irey was surprised when he was called before Secretary of the Treasury Andrew Mellon in the spring of 1929 and told that he had the full responsibility for apprehending Al Capone. To Irey, it seemed that any investigation of Al Capone should be undertaken by the

Justice Department, not the Treasury. Capone was a gangster, a killer, an extortionist and a court corrupter, all of which should have come under the jurisdiction of the Bureau of Investigation. He soon learned, however, the reasons for his special assignment. Citing the Manley Sullivan case, J. Edgar Hoover had manipulated the load from Justice onto the shoulders of the Treasury, and for a very good reason: he did not want to accept the responsibility if Capone could not be stopped. Naturally, Justice would be eager to prosecute, but if the evidence did not stick, Irey's unit would have to take the full blame.

Irey confronted the situation, but later observed painfully: "The task of putting Alphonse Capone in the penitentiary presented some rather obvious problems. . . . In the first place, the city of Chicago, Cook County, and the State of Illinois, whose citizens had had so much of their blood spilled by Alphonse, had shown no disposition to do anything *but admit they were shocked.*"

Without the help of the local citizenry, who were too terrified to cooperate, or local politicians and police, who had been bribed into submission, Irey had only the barest outline of a plan. It was the most delicate moment of his career. Not only might a wrong decision ruin his chances of ever getting anything on Capone, but if he failed, the Intelligence Unit could easily be discredited. The agent chosen to spearhead an undercover investigation would have to be someone who was so thorough in his methods that he could be counted on to ferret out the slightest shred of evidence.

But with Secretary Mellon breathing down his neck, and President Hoover breathing down Mellon's, Elmer Irey wasted no time.

Frank Wilson, five feet eight inches tall and weighing 180 pounds, was a jaunty-appearing young man with a pointed cleft chin and a ready, affectionate smile. He had heavy eyebrows and long eyelashes behind the thin black-rimmed glasses he wore to correct his near-sightedness. His professional attire consisted of dark gray pin-striped suits, white shirts with starched collars, and thin-knotted neckties. To and from the office he wore a white Stetson with a large brim turned up in front in the current style.

His appearance was deceiving.

Irey's assistant, Harry Woolf, always felt intimidated by Wilson. He once remarked that if assigned to do so, Wilson would investigate his own grandmother. Woolf recalled an occasion when Wilson was sent to interview Hugh McQuillen, who was agent-in-charge in New York, in order to secure information on a tax evasion case. After speaking with Wilson, McQuillen called Woolf on the phone. Distraught because of the death of his wife just the week before, McQuillen asked Woolf to order Wilson to postpone the meeting. When Wilson refused Woolf's request, Woolf pleaded with him, suggesting that maybe he should question someone else now and return in a week or so to talk to McQuillen. Wilson called Woolf chicken-hearted; Woolf retorted that Wilson was too aggressive. A fierce argument erupted. But Wilson stood his ground.

Woolf, who characterized himself as a very soft-hearted individual who was sympathetic to people, found Wilson to be just the opposite—very aggressive and tough, and utterly ruthless when he went after something. However, Woolf later admitted that he admired Wilson very much.

Frank Wilson's reputation had spread to the underworld as well. "He sweats ice water," one criminal remarked after Wilson forced him to confess to a stolen securities charge.

But there was another side to Frank Wilson . . .

Three hundred miles away from the Greenpoint section of Brooklyn where Al Capone was born, grew up and established himself as a street-gang thug, another boy was stopped by his father from becoming a member of a gang. When John Wilson observed his eleven-year-old son associating with boys who were known delinquents, he withdrew Frank's savings and built the boys a barn which he turned into a gymnasium. Years later, Frank credited the fact that he had not become a criminal to his father's concern for him.

John Wilson's straitlaced toughness grew out of a boyhood spent in the country. When he was eighteen, he had left the farmlands of upper New York State to join the Buffalo Police Force. He tried to instill in his son Frank the principles he had learned—hard work, honesty, manliness. It is not difficult to understand why Frank loved his father, why he wanted to be like him.

In 1897, John Wilson was selected to personally guard President McKinley when he came to Buffalo to speak to the annual convention of Veterans of the Grand Army of the Republic. Sitting astride a frisky black mare, he rode alongside the presidential carriage, magnificent in his blue uniform with brass buttons and his gray helmet. Frank waited with his mother on Main Street for more than an hour to watch his father ride by. As the presidential carriage passed them, John Wilson's horse suddenly reared. Frank's mother screamed, but his father just smiled down at them, calmed the animal, and rode on.

Four years later McKinley returned to Buffalo to

attend the opening of the Pan-American Exposition, but on this occasion John Wilson was not among those assigned to guard him. On the afternoon of his arrival the President was shaking hands with well-wishers when a medium-sized man in his early thirties worked his way up through the stream of people and pumped two bullets into McKinley's stomach and chest.

The events that followed in the next few hours affected Frank Wilson's whole life.

News of the shooting spread like wildfire through the city of Buffalo. Rumors leaked out that the assassin, a Polish anarchist named Leon Czolgosz, had been taken to police headquarters, two blocks from the newspaper section of downtown Buffalo. Crowds formed, surging toward the downtown area, eager for a glimpse of the prisoner. In front of police headquarters a strong cordon of police drawn across the pavement met the advancing crowd head-on. It was admitted that Leon Czolgosz was inside.

The crowd's ringleaders began shouting:

"Lynch him!"

"Let's kill the bastard!"

"Put him in a boat and send him over Niagara Falls!"

On the edge of the crowd stood a thirteen-year-old boy with deep-set eyes in a very serious white-moon face. Though thin and not very tall, Frank Wilson had a well-developed chest, strong arms and large shoulders. He was a quiet boy. He would be a quieter man.

As Frank watched, intently studying the mob's fury, the crowd surrounding police headquarters continued to swell. By midnight it numbered two thousand. Officers from the station house tried to reason with the ringleaders, but without success.

Suddenly one of them screamed: "Rush the station!" Another joined in, "Drag the son of a bitch out here!" The mob burst forward.

At that moment, several patrol wagons pulled up.

As the extra reinforcements tried to subdue the crowd, Frank noticed a detail of a dozen or so blue-uniformed police—headed by an officer whom he recognized as his father's close friend, Captain John Martin—filing out of the station house.

In place of its usual ruddy, good-natured grin, Captain Martin's face wore a look of grim determination. Frank waved, but Martin did not seem to notice him as he herded his men into a police van. Seconds later, Frank watched the police van depart up Pearl Street.

Frank continued watching the crowd. By 2:00 A.M. it was completely out of control. Any second now it would rush the station house. The boy envisioned the massacre.

Then rumors began to fly. Word circulated that the assassin was no longer there: Czolgosz, disguised in a police uniform, had been spirited away in the police van under the direction of Frank's friend Captain John Martin.

Frank felt a vicarious thrill as he left the scene. From that moment on, the necessity for strong law enforcement was a motivating factor in his life. He had observed this driving force first in his father, then in Captain John Martin. He wanted to follow in their footsteps.

But when he graduated from Lafayette High School, Frank entered the real estate business instead. Then, in 1917, upon America's entry into the World War, Frank, like many other young men, rushed eagerly to enlist in the army. He was rejected, however, on the rifle range at Fort Niagara, New York. Noticing that Frank was aiming but couldn't seem to hit anything, the colonel in charge ordered him to direct his attention to a hill about half a mile away and tell him what he saw.

Frank squinted. "Two white horses, sir," he replied promptly.

"Those are cows," corrected the colonel dryly. "Report to the medical officer for an eye examination."

Frank guessed what was coming. He had faked his eye test to enlist; now it looked as though his nearsightedness were about to catch up with him.

The medical officer put up a chart a few feet in front of Frank's face and said, "Read."

Frank squinted. All he could make out was the enormous "E" at the top of the chart.

The medical officer promptly ordered an honorable discharge.

Frank left the army base, but he refused to give up. Hearing that the Canadian Army had relaxed its requirements for enlistees, he hastened by steamer across Lake Ontario and tried to enlist there. Again he was rejected.

Discouraged, Frank headed back home to Buffalo. But the desire to join the war effort remained. He began searching the newspapers, the bulletin boards in post offices and train stations. And then one day he opened the pages of the Buffalo *Standard* and saw an advertisement by the Treasury Department for criminal investigators.

Frank traveled by train to New York to take the civil service test. A week later he was notified that he had passed.

When America entered the World War, "food

[51]

mobilization" was recognized as her number-one obligation. Food reserves in Europe were reaching the vanishing point. German U-boats had sunk hundreds of ships carrying cargoes of food bound for France, Italy and England. Ten to twelve million European children were suffering from malnutrition. Starvation was taking a heavy toll in death and disease.

On May 5, 1917, Herbert Hoover was appointed by President Woodrow Wilson to head the American Food Administration. Supplementing President Wilson's detailed statement on the food challenge, Hoover issued a press release outlining the aims of his new agency:

The businessmen of this country, I am convinced . . . realize their own patriotic obligation and the solemnity of the situation, and will fairly and generously cooperate in meeting the national emergency. I do not believe that drastic force need be applied. . . . But if there be those who expect to exploit this hour of sacrifice, if there are men and organizations scheming to increase the trials of this country, we shall not hesitate to apply to the full the drastic, coercive powers that Congress has conferred upon us in this instrument.

The emphasis was on *voluntary* cooperation. Any war profiteers, however, would be tracked down and exposed. Such exposure would inevitably subject the guilty parties to public censure in the marketplace.

One of Hoover's first appointees was seventy-year-old James B. Stafford, who was named United States Food Administrator for northern and western New York State, with headquarters at Buffalo. Over six feet tall, with intense gray eyes and white hair, James Stafford was well known and highly respected, an industrious Buffalo businessman of unimpeachable integrity. His assignment was to expose war profiteers—either com-

[52]

panies or individuals taking advantage of the national emergency by creating shortages and raising prices. Stafford was pleased with the new young assistant assigned to him; Frank Wilson was intelligent and seemed like a hard worker.

Between Stafford and young Frank a close relationship grew, almost like that between father and son. Stafford encouraged Frank to go after all suspected violators of the Federal Food Administration Act, whether big or small.

While relief ships filled with staples were steaming toward Europe, Frank went to work in his home town, Buffalo. Originally he had reported to the Food Administration in New York City, but he had been transferred back to Stafford's office in Buffalo, and here, in the town where he had grown up, he knew exactly where to begin combing for leads, gathering details, picking up information for possible evidence. But as he began apprehending violators, Frank noticed that Stafford seemed unusually concerned about something. Stafford finally confided to him that if they followed the regular procedure with criminal cases—taking them through the United States district attorney for presentation to the United States commissioner, the grand jury and finally for prosecution in federal court—the war would be over before the majority of cases was even tried.

Besides, the immediate need was to focus publicity on the violators. Stafford prodded Frank to aim for the "big fish," believing that prosecution of big violators would in turn frighten the lesser ones into obeying the food laws. The bigger and more important the firms or individuals prosecuted, the less likely the little fellow would be to try to get away with a smaller crime.

To provide a blast of unfavorable publicity that

would result in loss of prestige and public patronage and thus keep potential hoarders and profiteers in line, Frank Wilson and James Stafford worked out their own system of hearings. Frank acted as prosecuting attorney, summarizing the case and presenting the evidence. Stafford then took over, chastising and shaming the merchants for their lack of patriotism. Although he had the power to revoke or suspend their licenses, Stafford generally concluded the informal hearings, which were always well attended by the press, by offering the violators the "alternative" of making a substantial voluntary donation to the Red Cross. The unfavorable publicity carried promptly by the newspapers, together with the falling away of the patronage of loyal citizens, was usually sufficient punishment even without the loss of a license. It also accomplished the prime purpose of discouraging potential violators.

In the beginning, Stafford and Frank ran the office alone. As their workload increased, they were assigned four more investigators and two stenographers. Frank was promoted to chief investigator and given full powers to prosecute any profiteer, big or little, until the war ended.

In spite of the success of their efforts, however, Stafford and Frank were well aware that they were skating on thin legal ice with their "informal" hearings. They had no real authority to force anyone to make a "voluntary" donation. If challenged, they had no law or ruling to fall back on.

Finally they met their match in an uncooperative millionaire who was hoarding sugar and flour. Two of Frank's investigators, acting on a tip, had found five barrels of each in the millionaire's barn under layers of hay. The violator turned up with his lawyer and defied the administrator, claiming that James Stafford had no right to hold such hearings or to force anyone to make a "voluntary" contribution.

Frank began feeling queasy. It was inevitable that their methods would be challenged, but now the prospect loomed that their administration might have no effectiveness at all.

At this point Stafford came up with a suggestion: "Let's see if we can get the United States Attorney to get a quick indictment. Then we can set the case for a prompt trial."

Frank's first appearance before a federal grand jury filled him with mixed feelings of wild joy and tremulousness. A chilly nervous tension took hold of him. He tugged at his tie, kept brushing his hair back out of his eyes with his fingers, incessantly tried to smooth the creases out of his coat as he sat listening, waiting.

The jury returned with an indictment.

Frank felt a surge of delight. James Stafford's idea had worked. They had found a new way to expose, intimidate and, if need be, prosecute food-law violators.

Shortly after the millionaire's case was tried, Frank began investigating one of America's most respected manufacturers.

Even though National Director Herbert Hoover had insisted on "complete self-effacement in this time of emergency," certain large companies still tried to exploit the public by selling frozen products as fresh. Frank received a tip from a wholesale dealer in Chippewa that Armour & Company was selling cold-storage butter which they were advertising as fresh and for which they were charging excessive prices. It was a clever profiteering gimmick. Cautioning Frank to build up a watertight case, Stafford told him: "A big corporation like that will fight us to the bitter end, so we must be absolutely certain that our case is sound." Neither man could have had any premonition of what the bitter end would be.

Frank started working. In one month he'd tracked down 370 sales in which retail dealers had received cold-storage butter after having paid fresh-butter prices. Frank was able to collect plenty of facts and information. Taking their case to the United States attorney, Frank and Stafford were assured that they were on solid ground, that their evidence definitely supported their charges.

The manager of the Buffalo branch of Armour & Company was notified to appear at a hearing one week later. Two days after this notice was delivered, Frank was approached by a newspaper reporter who knew him. "There's a top man from Armour & Company, Chicago, in town," the reporter informed him. "He called on a political boss to ask for some help on the case coming up for a hearing. What do you think the boss told him?"

"I can't imagine," Frank replied.

"He told him that Armour & Company might as well take its medicine, because nobody around here can fix or influence old man Stafford."

Frank's beaming grin of pleasure was wiped out by the remainder of the story. "The political boss then said, 'I'd like to help you—here's a suggestion. See Clark, Jones and Smith. They're attorneys for the bank that has a whopper of a mortgage on old man Stafford's building. He owes some back interest on the mortgage, and he's hard up for ready cash. They might be induced to put pressure on him.'"

Frank later discovered that the representative of Armour & Company had indeed retained the bank's law firm, Clark, Jones and Smith. A day later a member of the firm called on James Stafford. Adopting a man-to-man attitude, the attorney enjoined him, "Jim, you can't embarrass that fine old firm of Armour & Company by a public hearing. Suppose you let me make a donation to the Red Cross for them. I'll send it to the New York office to ward off any bad publicity in this area."

Stafford bristled. "What I say is that the case is a serious violation extending over a long period, and if there is to be one law for the little fellow and another for big firms such as Armour & Company, what good is either the law or the Food Administration?"

The lawyer lost no more time; he played his trump card. "You know our bank has been awfully easy with you."

Stafford was prepared, however, having been tipped off by Frank. It was no secret to anyone that he had gone into hock up to his ears over the building he owned in Buffalo. But both Armour and the firm of Clark, Jones and Smith had underestimated his stamina. He had no intention of being frightened into submission. "If your bank doesn't like the way I conduct this office, I'm sorry," Stafford replied coolly, "but we are at war. I require all small businesses to comply with the law, and I'll require the big ones to do so too."

Three days later Stafford received a telegram from the Legal Division of the Food Administration at Washington requesting that he and Frank appear there the following day for a conference on the Armour case. He told Frank to get the complete file together.

Upon arrival, they met with the Food Administration attorneys, who accorded them a courteous and respectful conference. But before leaving, the three courteous gentlemen suggested that perhaps it might be advisable to delay action on the case.

[57]

Stafford and Frank bolted out of the office and went immediately to Herbert Hoover. "I felt timid when we walked in," Frank remembered, "but in a couple of minutes my fear and nervousness vanished when confronted with Mr. Hoover's open, friendly smile and cordial greeting. A heavy-set, square-faced man, he had a lively sparkle in his eyes and a deliberate, unhurried manner." Unlike other men prominent in politics whom Frank had observed, Hoover didn't shuffle the papers on his desk or attempt to convey the impression that his visitors were using up his precious time.

Stafford and Frank gave Hoover a brief outline of the Armour case. Frank's heart leaped when Hoover raised his eyebrows at the mention of Armour and promptly became very interested. "I'll talk to the Legal Division about the case," Hoover promised.

At a second conference with the Food Administration lawyers, no mention was made of their previous suggestion to delay. On the contrary, they now seemed very enthusiastic and authorized Stafford to proceed.

The hearing was held later that month in Buffalo, and Armour & Company was found guilty.

Stafford announced that Armour could make a "voluntary" contribution of $5,000 to the "Free Milk Fund for the Babies of France"; otherwise the company would face suspension of its license. Armour appealed Stafford's decision to the United States Food Administration in Washington, but the decision was sustained by Hoover's office.

The Food Administration license of Armour & Company to deal in butter and eggs at their Buffalo branch was suspended for three months. It was customary procedure in such instances to tack on the door of the offending licensee a large cardboard sign announcing in red letters: LICENSE SUSPENDED—UNITED STATES FOOD ADMINISTRATION. Frank had the enormous satisfaction of being assigned by Stafford to tack up such a sign at Armour. But instead of only one sign, he took with him five, and gleefully nailed them securely at various prominent spots on the premises.

The next day James Stafford received from the bank a formal foreclosure notice demanding prompt payment of the entire amount of his mortgage plus interest. Desperately, he tried to raise a second loan on his building, but his attempts failed. Hounded by the bank's attorneys, he was finally forced to sell the building at a tremendous loss in order to meet their payment demands. For his equity, Stafford received only about $1,500. A local realtor estimated that the forced sale cost him approximately $100,000. Stafford's insistence on fulfilling his duty as United States Food Administrator for Buffalo had wiped out his entire life's savings.

Despite his personal tragedy, Stafford strongly encouraged his young assistant: "Frank, your forte is investigative work. I urge you to continue it. I'll guarantee you will never regret it."

Shortly thereafter, Frank was enlisted as a special agent in the Intelligence Unit of the Internal Revenue Bureau, under the direction of Elmer L. Irey.

In the decade that followed, Stafford's prediction proved true: Frank's passion for investigative work was all-consuming. But the exuberance and naïve impressibility of his early years had been replaced by a sheer, cold ruthlessness. He became obsessed with trial work. He relished going back again and again over the same documents, receipts, records—perhaps for the thousandth time—to indict someone, or to compel him to testify. He was an expert at breaking down witnesses. His methods were often brutal. One of them, the "bench treatment," consisted of stationing a defiant witness on a bench outside the grand jury room hour after hour, day after day, "waiting to be called." Frank tersely noted, "It's surprising how their memories improved under such circumstances—especially the most active, outdoor types." Elmer Irey soon came to regard Frank as his most effective investigator, using him to spearhead the department's most serious cases in all parts of the country.

Young ladies of the twenties wore thin dresses, short-sleeved and occasionally—in the evening— sleeveless. Many of them had abandoned their corsets. "The men won't dance with you if you wear a corset," they were heard to say. Among the new dances were the Charleston, the black bottom, the foxtrot, the shag, and other crazy ones that seemed to have sprouted up from nowhere. Bobbed-haired women with calf-length skirts were performing with their tuxedoed escorts such gyrations as the turkey trot, the grizzly bear, the bunny hug and the Castle walk, to the beat of "Tiger Rag," "Ja-da," "Dardanella," "Oh! How She Could Yacki, Hacki, Wicki, Wacki, Woo."

In Washington one hot afternoon in 1928, Frank Wilson left his office at the Treasury Department early. He had just returned to town after securing an indictment on a tax fraud case in St. Louis, and there were a few dance steps that were giving him trouble. He didn't have a steady girlfriend, but when he wasn't working, he was one of the town's most active bachelors. The frantic night life in the nation's capital required that he have more than a passing knowledge of the tango and the

Charleston. Outside of Washington, he conducted his private life in a tough, professional manner. But when he was working out of the office at 1111 Constitution Avenue, he loved to dance and to go to parties.

The dancing school he chose that particular afternoon agreed to furnish him with a private lesson. Frank did so well that he asked for another that evening. No private instructor was available, so the owner made a suggestion. He would ask the Women's City Club, which was having a class that evening, if they would permit Frank to take his class with them.

The Women's City Club was overjoyed; they agreed to let the young treasury agent join them.

At 7:00 P.M. the Women's City Club arrived at the school for their dance class. Frank's first partner on the floor was a cool, sparkling young redhead named Judith Barbaux. They danced the tango, the two-step, and finally the foxtrot. She told him that she worked as a secretary in the Defense Department; that her father, a Parisian, worked for the Department of State; that her mother was an American of Irish descent. She appeared to be spirited, lovable and spoiled. When they weren't dancing, Frank couldn't take his eyes off her.

Frank and Judith began meeting, going out for dates. Judith was curvaceous, petite, barely five feet tall; she was quick-witted and outspoken, two qualities that intrigued Frank tremendously. She would come right out and say whatever was on her mind. She was self-centered and very feminine, with strong opinions about everything. She was, Frank recollected, "the loveliest, most graceful and animated girl it had ever been my privilege to know."

It was an old-fashioned romance. They were married a few months later. Shortly afterward, Frank was promoted by the Treasury Department to a permanent position: agent-in-charge in Baltimore. He and Judith bought a tiny yellow cottage on the outskirts of the city.

Frank settled down and became utterly domestic. He spaded the yard surrounding the cottage and set out beds of roses and azaleas. He built feeders for the cardinals, blue jays, thrushes and squirrels that gathered around their front door. Both Frank and Judith were eager for a family. Tucked away in their little home, they prepared for a life of undisturbed tranquillity.

PART II

"He fears nothing that walks; he will sit quietly looking at books eighteen hours a day, seven days a week, forever, if he wants to find something in those books. He is soft-spoken and unemotional. Only the endless stream of nickel cigars he massacres keeps him from being a paragon of virtue."

—from Elmer L. Irey's private notes, describing Frank Wilson.

5
GET CAPONE

Frank did not tell Judith anything. When they started out for Chicago, he peered earnestly into her blue eyes, brushed back a lock of her red hair, and said in the most controlled voice he could manage, "Sweetheart, I'm after a fellow named Curly Brown. The government says we've got to put him away." He neglected—intentionally—to tell her that "Curly Brown" was an alias for Al Capone.

Elmer Irey's request that he lead the Capone investigation filled him with tremendous anxiety concerning Judith's safety. The fears gnawed at him. He knew what would happen when he began forcing inroads into the Capone machine; he could picture Capone ordering his henchmen to shoot both of them on sight.

He and Judith had been married a year. They had just gotten settled into their little cottage in Baltimore when Irey summoned him into his office and told him to proceed to Chicago at once. Frank admitted later, "Nothing could have been further from our Baltimore idyll."

Judith, in fact, did not have the slightest inkling of

[65]

the true identity of the man Frank was after. She did remark to him that she had never even heard of Curly Brown, to which Frank countered that Curly Brown's reputation was growing. Soon, he said, people would be hearing a great deal about him.

It was a dangerous deception. It could have seriously disturbed the basic trust they shared. But Frank felt there was no other way to protect the woman he loved.

Arriving in the cold, windy city of Chicago, he and Judith checked into three rooms at the Sheridan Plaza Hotel. It was a tremendous letdown from the little yellow cottage surrounded by roses and azaleas back home in Baltimore. But Judith forced herself to adjust, consoled by the knowledge that they would be returning home soon, when Frank had tracked down Curly Brown.

Irey gave Frank his choice of any of the agents in his department to assist him. Frank asked for the hawk-eyed Nels Tessem, already well known as a fearless investigator; William Hodgins; Clarence Converse; James N. Sullivan (of the New York office); and Michael F. Malone. For his base of operations, the government assigned him a room in Chicago's old Post Office Building—tiny, unventilated, with a cracked glass at the door, no windows, a double flat-topped desk, and peeling green walls.

As soon as they arrived, Frank began prowling the gang-run streets of Cicero. The challenge that confronted him was to find evidence that Capone's gross income exceeded $5,000 (the standard deduction at that time)—a formidable endeavor, as Capone had a habit of never signing or endorsing anything. It was as if he were anticipating the day he would be called on to answer for all the property he owned, all the money he had illicitly

[66]

earned. Capone did not maintain a bank account; he paid cash for everything. He never acquired property under his own name; he endorsed no checks, signed no receipts.

Irey's unit had developed two methods to trap taxpayers who concealed income. The first method involved analyzing a taxpayer's "net worth"; the second dealt with his "net expenditure." In the former method, a dollar value was placed on the taxpayer's scale of living and any outward evidences of his wealth. If these indicators were incommensurate with the individual's income, the Intelligence Unit assumed that he had increased his "net worth" by an unreported amount; this gain was then declared taxable. The second method applied the same yardstick to the taxpayer's running expenses, without regard to his accumulated assets.

In the case of Capone, Frank used both methods. He began searching Chicago for shops, real estate agents or establishments of any kind where Capone might have dealt. Proprietors were at first uncooperative, but Frank, using his toughest manner, finally persuaded several of them to supply figures of transactions. He questioned hotel clerks; pored over department store credit accounts; exhaustively analyzed the telephone company's records, cross-checking various numbers which he knew were Capone's. Gradually he compiled a partial list of Capone's outlay for goods and services during the years 1926 through 1929, together with evaluations of his fixed possessions. From two furniture companies Frank discovered that Capone had ordered $26,000 worth of chairs, sofas, tables, beds and rugs for his Prairie Avenue and Palm Island homes and his brand-new headquarters in the Hotel Lexington. Capone's custom-made suits; his silk monogrammed shirts, shorts, undershirts, pajamas

[67]

and handkerchiefs; his detachable stiff collars and his flannel winter underwear—most of it from Marshall Field & Company—came to about $7,000. Two Chicago jewelers had sold him $20,000 worth of silverware, a gold-plated dinner service, and personal ornaments, including thirty diamond-studded belt buckles. His Chicago hotel bills amounted to $1,500 a week. His telephone bills totaled $39,000. On the night of the Dempsey-Tunney fight, he had hosted a party that had cost $3,000. He traded in a 1924 McFarland town car, for which he had paid $5,500, in order to buy a more expensive new model. He also purchased a $5,000 Lincoln limousine. Tracing every available source, Frank uncovered $165,000 of taxable income.

But this did not satisfy Frank. It was a trivial sum in view of the millions that flowed to Capone from illicit businesses. Furthermore, the legality of the net worth–net expenditure principle as a basis for a criminal conviction had never been tested in a federal court. Prodded by Elmer Irey, Frank knew that his only course to ensure the kind of prison sentence President Hoover wanted for Capone was to dig up irrefutable evidence linking Capone to his gambling houses, brothels and distilleries.

Frank was sent to Chicago as "Special Agent-in-Charge of the Unit to Investigate the Income Tax Delinquencies of Alphonse Capone." Assigned to assist him was the Internal Revenue's Chicago agent-in-charge, A. P. Madden. Madden had privately confided to Frank that hanging an income tax rap on Alphonse Capone was going to be as easy as hanging a foreclosure sign on the moon. The following excerpt is from a report that Madden provided him after his arrival, vividly summarizing the situation in Chicago:

Get Capone

In 1924, in Chicago and vicinity, there were sixteen assassinations charged to the warring factions seeking control of underworld enterprises. In 1925, there were 46. In 1926, there were 64. In 1927, 1928 and 1929 the assassinations continued and became increasingly spectacular. It was obvious that many of the murders were due to Capone's determination to maintain territory which he had acquired and also to extend his authority into new areas. The machine-gun was introduced. It had come to be a common occurrence for a man, or a group of men, to be killed by machine-guns planted in the windows of lodging houses, in locations where it was known that the intended victims would some time appear. However, the assassinations were not always perpetrated by hired gunmen in hiding. One spectacular killing occurred at noon, at the intersection of Dearborn and Madison Streets, almost at the center of Chicago's downtown shopping district.

At various times, it appeared that Capone was seeking control over territory in the north and west sections of the city of Chicago. There was evidence of working agreements with organizations which operated in those sections, but he never gained complete control over them. For a considerable period prior to 1929, liquor and other underworld enterprises in an extensive area in the north section of Chicago were controlled by George "Bugs" Moran, a resourceful and desperate individual, with a long criminal record. On February 14, 1929, seven of Moran's associates were assassinated at one time in a garage on North Clark Street. That crime was committed at about 10:00 A.M. No one was ever prosecuted in connection with it, and virtually all of the other gang murders went unsolved. It was obvious that Capone's police connections and his political influence, not only in the city but in the suburbs, were such as to make him immune from conviction, and even prosecution.

For reasons which cannot, on account of lack of space, be set forth in detail, Capone, about 1924, moved his headquarters from the Hawthorne Hotel in Cicero to the Metropole Hotel in Chicago. The Metropole Hotel is located at Michigan Avenue and 23d Street, and for many years was a respectable

[69]

residential establishment. When Capone moved in with his headquarters organization, he took over a considerable part of the hotel. His principal assistants were then Ralph Capone, his brother, who had charge of vice, and to some extent, supervised the sale of beer; the Guzik brothers, headed by Jack Guzik, who was largely in charge of gambling operations and political and police "fixing"; Frank Nitti, known in newspaper parlance as the "Enforcer," who had charge of alcohol; Johnny Patton, the Mayor of the Village of Burnham, who had wide political influence and was involved in many forms of underworld activities in the southwestern suburbs; Denis Cooney, known as the "Duke," a proprietor of disorderly resorts and long a figure of importance in the First Ward; Tony Lombardo, a power in the Unione Siciliane; "Machine Gun" Jack McGurn, whose real name was Gebhardi; and Frank Rio, a gunman. One of Capone's close associates was a member of the cabinet of William Hale Thompson, who succeeded Mayor Dever in office. There were members of the State Legislature who, rightfully or wrongfully, were regarded as his representatives. It was frequently stated that there were members of Congress who were under his control. The head of the Chicago Crime Commission addressed a letter to Senator William E. Borah, chairman of a sub-committee of the Judiciary Committee of the Senate, in which he alleged that a member of the staff of the United States Attorney was a Capone partisan.

After maintaining his headquarters at the Metropole Hotel for a year or two, Capone moved his organization to the Lexington Hotel, located at Michigan Avenue and 22d Street. In that hotel he occupied most of three floors. Gunmen patrolled the lobbies and corridors. Members of the organization were located in rooms across the street from the hotel and at various places in the neighborhood. Capone was then known internationally. He was set up in the public mind as the symbol of organized crime. The Chicago newspapers and various civic organizations were demanding relief from an intolerable situation. Gang murders continued . . . and the indications were that Capone had corrupted and gained control of a considerable part of the law enforcement machinery of Chicago and Cook County.

[70]

. . . in connection with his appearance before the subcommittee of the Judiciary Committee of the United States Senate, referred to above, District Attorney George E. Q. Johnson of Chicago stated: "I just selected here from my memoranda a case which will help the Senators better to understand the conditions under which we had to work, and what confronted the court—here was an indictment for conspiracy, D.C. 14677. There were 31 defendants. Six of these defendants were murdered—I do not suppose their names would be of any interest—before the case came to trial, and eight were murdered who were associated with them, and some were prospective witnesses."

Capone had developed beyond the point where he merely controlled a large part of the beer, liquor, gambling and vice enterprises in this vicinity. While the Chicago newspapers were simultaneously glorifying and attacking him, they called him in to settle a newspaper strike. He was gradually acquiring some control of labor organizations. The cleaning and dyeing industry was seething with violence, and one of the prominent proprietors of a large cleaning and dyeing establishment took Capone in as a partner. Other instances of this general character could be furnished if space were available.

Late in 1929, I was talking to the Commissioner of Police of the City of Chicago, in his office. I reminded him of the fact that if an accident occurred in the street and a crowd gathered in such a way as to obstruct traffic, the police officers would disperse the crowd peacefully if they could, but forcibly if they must. I asked him if the police, in the ordinary exercise of their authority, could disperse a crowd on the street, why they could not and did not break up a criminal organization that maintained flamboyant headquarters in a well-known city hotel. I suggested driving the organization from the Lexington Hotel, and from any other point within the limits of the city where it might congregate. The Commissioner, whose own intentions I believed were good, listened with attention. He stated that he would like to discuss the matter with me at some later date when more time was available. He did not say so, but I distinctly gained the impression that, so far as the Capone organization was concerned, he would not be permitted to take the direct action which he himself probably was disposed to take.

It was a perilous task that lay before Frank and the other agents of the Intelligence Unit. It appeared probable that if they could not find a way to stop Capone, Capone would never be stopped. Frank's leads had already begun to dwindle. He tried to find some other means to link Capone with his business interests, his vast holdings. As he remembered, "I legged it to the banks and credit agencies trying to find some record of business transactions involving Scarface [Capone]. Not a tumble. I prowled the crummy streets of Cicero, where a twitch of Al's little finger had the force of an edict, but there was no clue that a dollar from the big gambling places, the horse parlors, the brothels or the bootleg joints ever reached his coffers. . . . I was stuck, bogged down. . . . Judith (who was dying to go back to Baltimore) kept saying, 'You're certainly making a mountain out of this Curly Brown case. He can't be such a big shot. I never see a word about him in the newspapers.' But Capone was all over the front pages every day. It was common talk that he got a cut on every case of whiskey brought into Cook County; that he ran a thousand bookie joints, fifteen gambling houses, a swanky string of brothels; that he controlled half a dozen breweries. He had bought himself a Florida palace on Palm Island, imported a chef from Chicago and was spending $1,000 a week on banquets. He tore around in sixteen-cylinder limousines, slept in $50 French pajamas, and ordered fifteen suits at a time at $135 each. His personal armed forces numbered 700, equipped with automatic weapons and armored automobiles. And I couldn't show that this satrap of Chicago earned more than $5,000 a year! Evidence of lavish living wasn't enough. The courts had to see *income*."

"Frank, I want you to get Al Capone!" Irey's order to him had been handed straight down from the White House.

"That was all I had to do," Frank recalled grimly, "just—go get Al Capone."

Jake Lingle was a sixty-five-dollar-a-week crime reporter for the Chicago *Tribune*. He was close to Al Capone. He wore one of the diamond belt buckles Capone gave to people he liked. He was a guest several times at Capone's Palm Island estate. But it was all ostensibly part of his job.

Frank, however, suspected otherwise.

Checking, Frank learned that Lingle had just turned twenty when he went to work for the *Tribune* as a copyboy. Lingle, a solidly built man of medium height, with curly black hair, ruddy cheeks and a cleft chin, could radiate a certain boyish charm. After only a few weeks on the *Tribune*, he had talked his way into being assigned to a police reporter's beat.

Lingle was a legman. He had no special aptitude for writing, but he could transmit facts, and he often scooped the competition. The *Tribune* soon regarded him as one of its more valuable assets. Crime was daily front-page news in the Chicago of the twenties, and the *Tribune* began to rely heavily on its house crime expert, its "gangologist."

And by this time, Jake Lingle had gained direct access to Al Capone.

By the time he was thirty, Lingle not only owned a house on Chicago's West Side but had purchased a

[73]

summer bungalow at Long Beach, Indiana, for $18,000. In the winter he often took his wife and two children to Cuba or Florida for a vacation. He sped around town in a chauffeur-driven limousine. Lingle's one vice was gambling. He frequently risked $1,000 or more on a horse race.

Such extravagance for a sixty-five-dollar-a-week legman had puzzled his colleagues, but Lingle's coy explanation was that his father had bequeathed him $50,000. Also, he maintained, the value of some stocks he had bought during the 1928 bull market had almost tripled.

Frank checked it out and found that Lingle's story was a lie. Probate records showed that the senior Lingle had left his son not $50,000, but less than $500. Frank then investigated the four brokerage houses where Lingle kept trading accounts. He learned that if Lingle had liquidated his securities at the peak of the bull market in September 1929, he could have profited by $85,000, but he had held onto them. On October 24— Black Thursday—the paper profit plus $75,000 more of Lingle's money had evaporated.

Yet Lingle had not lowered his standard of living— in fact, he had raised it. He had on deposit in the Lake Shore Savings and Trust Bank a total of $63,900.

From underground sources, Frank learned that "Jake is a fixer." It was well known that Lingle had strong friends in the police department. There were other rumors that he was the liaison between the Capone organization and City Hall—the bag man.

Frank knew that if he could get Lingle to cooperate, he might be the key that could link Capone directly to the big gambling places, horse parlors, brothels and bootleg joints under his control.

Aware of *Tribune* publisher Robert McCormick's antipathy for Capone, Frank called on McCormick at his office. He informed him that Jake Lingle's help would be greatly appreciated by the United States Government.

"I'll get word to Lingle to go all the way with you," McCormick promised him.

At noon the next day, Jake Lingle started for the Washington Park race track in Homewood, Illinois. It was a brilliantly sunny day, with a clear blue sky overhead. It was much too beautiful a day to be riding inside a chauffeur-driven limousine, so Lingle dismissed his car and pursued his way jauntily across Wacker Drive toward the suburban station of the Illinois Central Railroad on Randolph Street and Michigan Avenue. He had almost an hour to spare before the 1:30 race track special left the station. He decided to take a slight detour for a bite of lunch in the coffee shop of the Hotel Sherman. Entering the lobby, he ran into a police sergeant friend, Tom Alcock. Lingle remarked, "I'm being tailed." But he did not appear troubled.

After having a bite of lunch, he started out again for the Illinois Central Station. He stopped at the newsstand in front of the public library to buy the *Daily Racing Form*. A man he knew called him from a car parked next to the curb: "Play Hy Schneider in the third, Jake."

Lingle grinned. "I've got him."

Lighting a cigar, he hurried down the stairs into the pedestrian tunnel running under Michigan Avenue toward the station, where he was suddenly surrounded by swarming crowds. He snapped open the racing form and began reading intently, oblivious of the pushing and shoving of the noontime throng. Neither did he notice the tall blond man behind him who, in his haste, was

[75]

elbowing people out of the way, trying to catch up with him.

As Lingle arrived at the east ramp, the tall blond man fetched up close to him, drew a .38 caliber Colt revolver and leveled it only inches from the back of the reporter's head.

The sudden force of the bullet that plowed through Lingle's brain rammed his head forward. He toppled over, still clutching the racing form in his hand, the burning cigar crushed between his lips as his eyes and nose slammed against the cement platform.

A dozen people gasped. The blond killer dashed back toward the stairway at the opposite end of the tunnel, then up the stairs, two or three at a time, jostling a man coming down. He paused a second at the top as a woman screamed, "Isn't anybody going to stop him?" Her husband leaped up the stairs; others joined in the chase, across the ramp toward Randolph Street, the killer darting through a twisting maze of alleys. He vanished, seconds later, swallowed by the crowd.

The following morning, the nation's press reacted with cold astonishment. Harry Chandler, the president of the American Newspaper Publishers' Association, praised Lingle as "a first-line soldier" in the war against organized crime. The *Tribune* joined in:

The meaning of this murder is plain. It was committed in reprisal and in an attempt at intimidation. Mr. Lingle was a police reporter and an exceptionally well informed one. His personal friendships included the highest police officials, and the contacts of his work made him familiar to most of the big and little fellows of gangland. What made him valuable to his newspaper marked him as dangerous to killers.

It was all too trumped up for Frank Wilson. He

decided it was now time to blow the lid on the press and to point a finger at Capone. He conferred with John T. Rogers of the St. Louis *Post-Dispatch*, a reporter whom Frank had once helped win a Pulitzer Prize by supplying him with the information he needed to expose a corrupt federal judge. Wilson released to Rogers the details he had uncovered on Lingle.

Colonel McCormick nearly exploded when he read Rogers's article the following morning.

Finally, one week later, the *Tribune* was forced to run a second major editorial on the Lingle case.

When Alfred Lingle was murdered, the motive seemed to be apparent . . . his newspaper saw no other explanation than that his killers either thought he was close to information dangerous to them or intended the murder as notice given the newspapers that crime was ruler in Chicago. . . .

Alfred Lingle now takes a different character, one in which he was unknown to the management of the *Tribune* when he was alive. He is dead and cannot defend himself, but many facts now revealed must be accepted as eloquent against him. . . . The reasonable appearance against Lingle now is that he was accepted in the world of politics and crime for something undreamed of in his office and that he used this in undertakings which made him money and brought him to his death.

A severe blow was dealt to journalistic pride. The press took for granted that its reporters and writers were above the corruptive control of the underworld. Now the public was asking, How many other newspapermen do the gangsters own?

A few weeks later, a St. Louis reporter, Harry T. Brundige of the *Star*, conducted a four-hour interview with Al Capone at his Palm Island estate.

BRUNDIGE: I thought I'd ask you who killed Jake Lingle.

CAPONE: Why ask me? The Chicago police know who killed him.

BRUNDIGE: Was Jake your friend?

CAPONE: Yes, up to the very day he died.

BRUNDIGE: Did you have a row with him?

CAPONE: Absolutely not.

BRUNDIGE: How many rackets was Lingle engaged in? (Capone shrugged.) What was the matter with Lingle?

CAPONE: The horse races.

BRUNDIGE: How many Lingles are there in Chicago?

CAPONE: In the newspaper racket?

BRUNDIGE: How many reporters do you have on your payroll?

CAPONE: Plenty!

"Listen, Harry," Capone finally said, giving a hearty laugh and throwing a beefy arm around the reporter's shoulders, "I like your face. Let me give you a hot tip: Lay off Chicago and the money-hungry reporters. You're right, and because you're right, you're wrong. You can't buck it, not even with the backing of your newspaper, because it's too big a proposition. No one will ever realize just how big it is, so lay off. They'll make a monkey out of you before you get through. No matter what dope you give that grand jury, the boys will prove you're a liar and a faker. You'll get a trimming."

"I'm going to quote you as saying that," Brundige warned.

"If you do, I'll deny it."

Both the *Star* and the *Tribune* published Brundige's interview. Capone immediately branded it a fabrication.

6
THE BUSINESSMAN AND THE DUDE

In the aftermath of Jake Lingle's murder, Capone made a grand gesture: he offered to help the police track down Lingle's killer. The story was picked up by the Chicago *Tribune*, and Frank forwarded the newspaper accounts to Elmer Irey.

I am enclosing articles appearing in the Chicago *Tribune* of April 20th and 21st, regarding the Lingle investigation. You will be interested in these stories because of their reference to Al Capone and his organization.

Frank had headed to St. Louis to visit *Post-Dispatch* John T. Rogers, the reporter who had disclosed to the world, with Frank's help, the true story of Jake Lingle. John Rogers and Frank met for lunch at the swank Missouri Athletic Club with a suave, good-looking gentleman whom Rogers introduced as a Mr. Edward O'Hare. O'Hare proved to be very talkative and filled with stories. He amused them both with anecdotes about his bright twelve-year-old son, Butch. Butch was set on going to the United States Naval Academy at Annapolis, and he wanted to be an admiral when he grew up. At one point O'Hare remarked, "If I never do another thing in my life, I'm going to see that that kid's wish to get into Annapolis is granted."

Later in the week, John Rogers phoned Frank. "I can put you in touch with a businessman who got sucked into the Capone syndicate. He's willing to help you."

"That's swell," Frank replied. "Who is he?"

"Eddie O'Hare, the gentleman you had lunch with. He wanted to look you over. He's satisfied."

"I hope he doesn't have too much blood on his hands and that we can depend on him."

"I've known him for twenty years," Rogers replied. "He never got drawn directly into any of the gang wars. He limits his activity to legitimate dog tracks and has no connection with the Capone booze and vice rackets. He has wanted for a long time to get away from Capone, but once the syndicate sucks in a businessman, they just don't let him retire."

Frank grew more cautious. "How come he's willing to work for me?"

"He's nuts about that boy Butch. He's dead set on getting him into Annapolis, and he figures he has to break away. But he can't do it while Capone is on the throne. I told him you were making headway, and that if he helped, the big shot might be on his way to the penitentiary a little quicker."

"Does he realize that in helping me put Scarface on the spot, he's taking his life in his hands?"

"Hell, Frank," Rogers replied, "if Eddie had ten lives to live, he'd jeopardize every one of them for that boy Butch."

Frank began checking on O'Hare. He learned that in

[80]

The Businessman and The Dude

1919 he had formed a partnership with Oliver P. Smith, the inventor of the mechanical rabbit used in dog racing. When Smith died in 1927, O'Hare obtained sole control of the patent rights.

Greyhound racing was at first illegal throughout the country, so the track owners who leased the rabbit from O'Hare were generally gangsters. As dog racing caught on in both America and Europe, O'Hare grew wealthy. Al Capone first became connected with O'Hare when he installed a mechanical rabbit at the Hawthorne Kennel Club, on the outskirts of Cicero.* O'Hare despised Capone, but he enjoyed the riches he poured on him. "You can make money through business associations with gangsters," he had once remarked, "but you will run no risk if you don't associate personally with them. Keep it on a business basis and there's nothing to fear."

But O'Hare *had* consorted personally with gangsters—from the very beginning.

When the Prohibition law was first passed, the government had permitted liquor wholesaler George Remus to store $200,000 worth of whiskey in the building where O'Hare was conducting his law practice. Shortly thereafter, all of this liquor found its way into bootleg markets in Chicago, New York and other cities. George Remus was furious. The liquor had been stolen from right under his nose, and he hadn't received a dime. He brought charges against O'Hare and twenty-one others. O'Hare was indicted and sentenced to one year in prison. The decision was reversed on appeal when Remus withdrew

---

* Various illegal practices were used by gangsters to trap unsuspecting bettors. Given eight greyhound entrants, for example, nothing was easier than to overfeed seven of them by a couple of pounds of meat, thus guaranteeing victory for the eighth dog. Another less subtle method involved running seven of the dogs a mile before the race, thus exhausting them so that the eighth dog couldn't lose.

[81]

his original testimony. O'Hare, it was learned later, had secretly made a deal to compensate Remus.

"Artful Eddie," as some of his colleagues referred to him, was an attractive, well-mannered young man. A superb athlete, he rode, swam, boxed, played golf; he never smoked and he drank no hard liquor. Married when he was a young man, he fathered two boys and a girl. His boy Edward H., Jr., a beautiful, blond-haired little fellow, was the apple of his eye—his beloved "Butch," whom he had boasted about to John Rogers and Frank over lunch at the Missouri Athletic Club. "My son Butch" were words O'Hare frequently repeated. More than anything, he wanted his boy to have an outstanding future.

O'Hare became more deeply involved with Capone when he tried to open a dog track of his own. He leased land near Capone's Hawthorne Kennel Club and inaugurated the Lawndale Kennel Club. It was a bold intrusion into Capone territory, but he was cautious. He let Capone know that if anybody attempted to harm him or put him out of business, he would withdraw the rights to the mechanical rabbit. If they didn't allow *him* to operate, *they* couldn't operate. Capone finally proposed the merger of the two tracks. O'Hare agreed.

In the twenties, the public was mad about dog racing, and Capone's syndicate was kept busy day and night building grandstands and pari-mutuel booths to keep pace with this overwhelming interest. Weekly profits often ran to more than $50,000. O'Hare presided as counsel and manager, a double function he executed with such skill that Capone's syndicate later entrusted him with its dog tracks in Florida and Massachusetts.

Frank telegraphed the following message to John Rogers:

The Businessman and The Dude

MR. JOHN ROGERS
C/O ST. LOUIS POST DISPATCH
ST. LOUIS, MO.

WILL BE IN ST. LOUIS THURSDAY MORNING.
PLEASE NOTIFY OUR FRIEND THAT I WISH
TO SEE HIM.

WILSON

That Thursday morning, when he and Frank met, O'Hare agreed to assist the United States Government in its campaign against Capone. Within a few days, Frank wrote Irey:

Since my last letter relating to the above-numbered case we have been directing our efforts in attempting to establish the connection of the taxpayer [Capone] with the Hawthorne Dog Track. We are convinced that he was connected and hope to establish it.

In order to protect this valuable insider, Frank refused to divulge, even to Irey, the identity of his "friend" in the Capone mob.

His memo continued:

Information was secured to the effect that Al Capone had an interest in the Hawthorne Kennel Club and that a large part of his income was derived from that source. It was alleged that although Capone was not a stockholder of record, he received a big cut from the proceeds of the track.

Upon my arrival in Chicago, I had a conference with Mr. Madden and the agents above mentioned, at which time we decided at once to make a most intensive investigation and examination of the business of the Hawthorne Kennel Club, as it was at that time by far the most primary lead to establish income of Capone. For about two months we devoted all our efforts in attempting to ascertain if any unreported proceeds of

[83]

the business had been diverted in any way to Capone or any other persons, and no evidence or information was found during our investigation to substantiate such reports.

All of the books, records and correspondence of the Hawthorne Kennel Club were turned over to our office and carefully checked in many ways; employees of the company were interviewed and a detailed search was made at various banks to learn whether any of the persons interested or associated with the track handled any funds which might come directly or indirectly from the proceeds of the track.

Because we found no trace of diverted proceeds, we were forced to close the angle of the Capone investigation, as it was our decision that no evidence existed to show unreported income of the Hawthorne Kennel Club. Changes were made in the tax liability of the corporation for some years because certain unallowable deductions had been made by it, but no effort had been made to conceal such payments.

Edward O'Hare agreed to continue working on the inside for Frank, and to relay to him any information he could safely lay his hands on. Frank knew, however, that he needed someone much closer to pose as an intimate of Capone and to telegraph Capone's every move back to him. He needed a man who was prepared to be murdered should his true identity be discovered.

Michael F. Malone was one of the agents Frank had requested from Elmer Irey. Barrel-chested and powerfully built, he carried 200 pounds on his five-foot-eight-inch frame. He had a beaming, exultant grin. With his jet black hair and sharp, biting brown eyes perpetually ringed by heavy dark circles, he could pass easily for Italian, Jew, Greek—whatever the occasion called for. He was in fact "black Irish" from Jersey City.

Malone had been injured while fighting in World War I when his airplane was forced down; he ended up marrying the nurse who attended him in the hospital. They had one child, a little girl, who was killed in a truck accident at the age of three.

After this tragedy, Mike and his wife drifted apart. He then joined the Intelligence Unit, where he seemed to lose interest in everything except undercover work. Malone didn't smoke or drink; he kept a room full-time at the St. Paul Hotel in St. Paul, Minnesota, although he hardly ever stayed there, as he was constantly on duty throughout the country. His friend, Special Agent Dick O'Hanlan, remembered Malone as being "tight-lipped, extremely careful, with a brilliant memory. He never forgot a thing." Frank Wilson went on to describe him as "the greatest natural undercover worker the Service has ever had."

Frank Wilson had been watching the supreme headquarters of Capone's syndicate, the Lexington Hotel. There, from a lavish sixth-floor suite, Capone masterminded the gang wars and executions and supervised his various illicit operations—the whorehouses, gambling joints, breweries, distilleries. From there Capone directed the manipulation of elections in Cook County and throughout Illinois, and ordered out his cadre of guerrillas to support—and, when necessary, to intimidate—the city, county and state officials on his payroll.

In addition to the large suite Capone used as an office, adjoining suites were assigned to his board of directors—Jack "Greasy Thumb" Guzik, generalissimo of the gambling and vice business; Ralph "Bottles" Capone, brother of Scarface, in command of the bootleg-liquor business; and Frank Nitti, "The Enforcer"—circled by at least a hundred other killers and strong-arm

[85]

Mafiosi, occupying dozens of other choice rooms in the building.

Frank recalled that "Mike Malone smiled widely when I suggested that he move into the Lexington."

Frank took him on a shopping spree to buy him some flashy gangster-looking clothes. He had him fitted out with a checked suit, half a dozen custom-tailored purple shirts, scores of hand-painted silver-and-gold neckties, and a white felt hat with a snap brim. Malone looked every bit the dandy, and he seemed truly disgusted with the role he had to play. It was as if the thought of having to put on gaudy gangster clothes bothered him more than getting his brains beaten out with a baseball bat.

A few days later, Malone headed for Brooklyn in order to brush up on his Italian. He hung around the tough neighborhoods of Greenpoint and Flatbush, picking up bits of information, gossip, nicknames of thugs and gangsters on their way up, anything that might aid him in developing his speech and gestures.

Finally, in a dingy Manhattan hotel room, Malone packed his bag. Into it went his purple shirts, most of them bearing the labels of Philadelphia haberdashers—and all of them bearing the marks of Philadelphia laundries—followed by garish-looking undergarments and a dozen Venetian silk pocket handkerchiefs embroidered with the crest "M.L." Shuddering with distaste, he clapped the white hat onto his head, pulled down the side brim, donned a light tan camel-hair overcoat, and headed for the terminal to catch a train for Chicago.

On arriving at his destination, Mike stepped into a phone booth, dropped a nickel into the coin slot, dialed a number, muttered into the receiver, "Frank, I'm here," and immediately hung up. He then hailed a taxi to take him to the Lexington Hotel. Signing the register "Michael Lepito," he was given room 724, right next to Phil D'Andrea, Capone's chief bodyguard. He had landed in the very center of the Capone ring.

Malone began hanging around the lobby of the Lexington. He asked no questions, merely sat quietly reading a newspaper. Occasionally he would join in a game of "Fourteen," a form of high-odds dice. He wrote a series of self-addressed letters and mailed them to friends in Philadelphia, who mailed them back. He was pleased when he discovered that the letters had been opened. Someone had also searched his room, inspecting the labels of his flashy new wardrobe.

As he continued to sit silently in the hotel lobby, reading and writing letters to himself, the flower of America's hoodlumhood marched before his eyes— "Machine Gun" Jack McGurn, "Tough Tony" Capeizzo, Jack and Sam Guzik, Paul Ricca, Frank "The Enforcer" Nitti, Louis Campaignia, known as "Little New York"—and Big Al himself.

One afternoon a Capone henchman known as Mike Kelly, a broad-faced thug with a thin grin, broke the silence with an offhand, "What's your line?"

It was the opening Malone had been waiting for. He peered at Kelly a moment, then drawled, "What's yours?"

Kelly hesitated, then answered, "I work around here."

Malone pretended to loosen up a bit. "My line is keeping quiet."

Kelly nodded. Then smiled. "Where you from?"

Malone pretended to give the question a good deal of thought. He had rehearsed the answer a hundred times, but it had to appear to come out with tremendous

[87]

reluctance. Softly, Malone explained, "Originally I'm from Brooklyn. I came out here from Philadelphia." Then in a burst of well-rehearsed confidence he continued: "I get jumpy sitting around indoors all the time. But I guess it's healthy."

Kelly walked away. Malone wondered where he was going, but there was nothing more to do but wait.

Gradually he worked his way into Kelly's confidence. After a couple of days, over a few drinks, Malone frankly admitted to Kelly that the Philadelphia cops were looking for him.

That evening Kelly invited him to play cards with some of the boys in a room off the lobby. The talk was free, and Malone soon started winning. Holding an unbeatable hand, he looked up suddenly into a face that made his blood run cold. It was Willie Heeney, beer-runner and all-around thug, whom Malone had personally arrested six years before. Heeney now stood directly across from him, watching him intently. Malone tried to shut out the image of himself encased in concrete, being hurled into the waters of Lake Michigan.

He wanted to get out of the room, to run. To his horror, his cards were good. He had drawn three sixes. If he hurriedly tossed in so powerful a hand, unplayed, the men surrounding the table would be suspicious. He had to play it out.

In a matter of seconds, his three sixes beat a pair of aces and a pair of jacks held confidently by "Golf Bag" Sam Hunt, the killer who had earned his unique nickname by transporting a Thompson submachine gun in a golf bag.

Malone speedily raked in the winnings. He had no other course now but to play a few more hands and wait to see what Heeney would do. After two more hands,

Malone quit, got up, walked to the newsstand, bought a newspaper, and sat down in the lobby. Pretending to read it, he peered at Heeney, who continued watching the play. Malone went for a quick walk around the block. When he returned to the Lexington, Heeney was still immersed in the game. Malone gave a sigh of relief; evidently Heeney hadn't remembered his arresting officer of half a decade before.

In the weeks that followed, Malone kept hanging around the Lexington, trying to pick up more information. He asked no questions, spoke only when he was spoken to, and behaved like a hoodlum minding his own business. When prompted, he would reminisce briefly about the good old days in Philadelphia and in the neighborhoods of Brooklyn. It didn't matter that some of the old-timers had never heard of him. Why should they expect him to be the only man in the Hotel Lexington using his real name? He seemed to know what he was talking about when he mentioned Philadelphia or Brooklyn detectives who were tough and uncooperative. He was up on new and old gang feuds; and, best of all, he knew who was whose girlfriend in the old neighborhoods.

Malone felt he was really "in" when one evening a drunken mobster began praising to him the wisdom of Big Al. "Al's a smart guy, all right. They ain't never goin' to get nothin' on him."

Malone agreed that Al was smart and that "they" certainly weren't ever "goin' to get nothin' on him."

The mobster kept talking. "Everything is businesslike. Take the Enforcer; he keeps everybody in line for Al. Somebody gets out of line, Al tells the Enforcer. The next thing you know, a couple of guys get off a train from Detroit or New York or St. Louis, and the

[89]

Enforcer tells them who has to go. The guys do the job and go home. When the guys from out of town louse up a job and only 'hurt' somebody, the Enforcer don't fool around. He has one of his own guys get the two guys who blew the job. That's why very few fellas get 'hurt' around here. They get killed."

The devoted mobster further emphasized his point by adding, "You guys in Philadelphia don't know how to do things in a businesslike way."

Malone humbly admitted that Philadelphia's underworld had produced nobody like Al Capone.

The drunken mobster went on: "Al don't like his guys to do no shootin' unless it's absolutely necessary. And then they gotta be quiet. That's what happened to Scalise and Anselmi." All that Malone—and, for that matter, anyone else—knew up to that point about Scalise and Anselmi was that they had been found atop a pile of rubbish a year before, beaten to death. The mobster took another drink and continued, "I don't want Al givin' me no banquets. I see him give a guy a banquet one night, and when the guy gets up to take a bow, Al reaches for a baseball bat and beats the guy's brains out right in front of everybody."

Once again Malone felt a twinge of terror pass through him.

As the weeks passed, Malone carefully kept his eyes and ears open. He contacted Frank regularly to give him a report over the phone. Occasionally, when he could shake the mob, he would turn up at Frank's apartment, where Judith would fix him a midnight meal.

But the image of Scalise and Anselmi being brutally beaten to death by the huge, bat-wielding figure of Al Capone never left his mind.

7
NITTI

The conditions under which a special agent for the Intelligence Unit had to function were much the same as those under which a field representative of any other governmental department had to operate. Expense accounts were closely scrutinized, and each item had to be accounted for. Frank directed the following memo to Elmer Irey:

Chief of the Intelligence Unit:

It is requested that authority be secured for me to travel on December 22 by my own auto from Washington, D.C. to Buffalo, N.Y. to Chicago, Illinois on cases————.

The authority for the use of my automobile is desired, as during the course of my investigations on the above-numbered cases it has been necessary to use my auto in locating witnesses in Chicago and vicinity. Many of the witnesses do not respond to letters, and without an auto, it would take a long time to locate them in order to secure their evidence; and if their statements are not secured within a reasonable time, the case may be jeopardized through the disappearance of witnesses.

Frank J. Wilson
Special Agent

Month after month Frank continued to tramp the South Side and Cicero, visiting scores of banks and credit agencies, probing for financial transactions involving Capone, keeping a sharp lookout for the faintest sign of Capone ownership, how money was channeled from speakeasy or gambling dive into the coffers of the syndicate. He questioned saloonkeepers, bookmakers and small-business owners as well as bank tellers, auditors and accountants. Some of them he subpoenaed. Very few showed up for hearings. A year passed.

"Unusual difficulties were encountered," he wrote Irey, "because all important witnesses were either hostile to the government and ready to give perjured testimony in order to protect the leaders of their organization, or they were so filled with fear of the Capone organization . . . that they evaded, lied, left town and did all in their power to prevent the government from using them as witnesses. . . . In order to locate them and serve them with subpoenas, it was necessary to pick them up on the streets near Capone headquarters at the Lexington Hotel, at Cicero hotels and at nightclubs, also through various subterfuges."

Frank was gradually realizing that he was facing a city overwhelmed by fear. Trying to get people to testify against Capone took all the ingenuity he could muster. One prominent Chicagoan told him bluntly, "Why, Mr. Wilson, if I tell you about my deals with Capone, he'll have me taken for a one-way ride." Another witness, a broad-shouldered, six-foot Italian, seventy years old, went into hysterics when Frank called him in for a hearing. He showed up, accompanied by his wife, sobbing and trembling. "For God's sake, let me alone. They kill me if I talk. . . ."

"Who do you mean by 'they'?" Frank asked.

Drawing close to Frank, the tall Italian whispered, "They—the Mafia! The Black Hand torpedoes murder anyone who squeals on them—thirty years ago they cut the throat of my wife's brother in New York. To get away from the Black Hand we move to Cleveland and then to Chicago. We pray that they don't hurt us or our children—our padres in church beg us to pray that the Mafia will not keep disgracing us and our country. And Mr. Wilson, please, you watch out, because Capone might get them after you."

Frank learned of an elusive associate of Capone's named O'Dwyer. Further checking revealed that O'Dwyer played golf on weekends at a certain country club on the outskirts of the city. Frank and Judith drove out and parked near the entrance of the club to see if Frank could spot him. Judith still had no notion that Frank was after Capone; she still thought he was chasing the elusive Curly Brown. On this particular day Judith took some needlepoint, and Frank took along a book to read. They sat there waiting all Saturday afternoon, with no luck.

Early on Sunday morning they returned. About 11:00 A.M. a huge sport Cadillac drove up with four tough-looking characters. Frank experienced a throb of excitement as he murmured to Judith, "I'll bet that tall one is our baby." A few minutes later Frank drifted in to look at the register. He almost cheered when he saw O'Dwyer's name.

Returning, he told Judith that the man he was after was out on the links. Pulling their green DeSoto over, Frank parked next to the big Cadillac.

About one o'clock Judith announced dramatically that she was starving to death. As Frank recalled, "This was just the opening I needed to get her out of the way

[93]

until after I served the subpoena on O'Dwyer." Using all his powers of persuasion, he tried to coax her to go ahead to the hotel without him. With that, Judith promptly banished all thought of hunger and said flatly, "Those four gangsters might try to beat you up. I'm sticking right here with you."

Frank chuckled to himself, wondering what Judith could possibly do in a mix-up with four gangsters.

When he spotted the four thugs leaving the clubhouse, Frank leaped from the car and approached them, calling out, "O'Dwyer!" The tallest man turned, and Frank thrust the subpoena at him.

To Frank's surprise O'Dwyer snatched the subpoena, then turned on him. "I'm gonna break your goddamned—"

Judith had been taking it all in from the car. When he got as far as "break your goddamned," she pressed down hard on the DeSoto's horn and held it there. The blast was terrific. Immediately, members of the club came running out the front door. O'Dwyer hesitated. Two of his henchmen had already drawn revolvers. Seeing the other members pouring out of the clubhouse, O'Dwyer quickly motioned to his men. "Let's get going." They piled into the Cadillac and drove off. Frank, giving a long sigh of relief, turned and smiled at Judith.

Frank decided that the only way to loosen the tongues of witnesses was to close in on some of the big shots surrounding Capone. If he could pin an income tax violation on one of them, it would prove to others that the government meant business. Convening his agents, Frank ordered them to go after the number-two man in the Capone organization—Frank "The Enforcer" Nitti.

Nitti, a onetime barber, had, like his boss, come to Chicago from Brooklyn. He had started off humbly enough, brewing bootleg alcohol when he wasn't cutting hair. His progress in the Capone mob was rapid. In a short time he became second only to Capone himself, charged with keeping discipline within the mob. It was in this capacity that Nitti had earned the title "The Enforcer." His talents and tactics illustrated that he well deserved his title.

Special Agent Michael Malone, stationed at the Lexington Hotel, was getting very close to Nitti. In hurried phone calls he had started feeding vital information about the Enforcer to Frank. One evening Malone received from Big Al himself a personal invitation to a banquet, ostensibly to celebrate Nitti's birthday.

He immediately telephoned Frank from a pay phone around the corner from the Lexington. "This is Malone, Frank. Capone's giving a party. I've been invited."

"You going?"

"Sure. I ought to learn a lot."

Frank was alarmed. He was aware of Capone's reputation for throwing a banquet prior to batting out the brains of disloyal followers. He cautioned Malone about this, but Malone retorted, "Yeah, I know. But I'm going."

"Well, carry a gun, Mike, so if that big slob gets you up on the platform, at least you'll have a chance."

"That's impolite, Frank. You know you gotta check your gun at the door at Al's parties."

"Where's the party going to be?" Frank was growing more uneasy.

"Across the street at the New Florence Restaurant."

"Okay. I'll get Nels Tessem, and we'll park as close to the place as possible. If we hear any shooting, we'll try to get in there to help you."

[95]

"What'll I shoot with, Frank? Gotta check my gun at the door."

"Take two guns and check one."

"That's a great idea. I'll do it. So long."

Malone returned to the Lexington Hotel and picked up his hoodlum acquaintance Mike Kelly, and together they headed across the street to the banquet. Meanwhile, Frank and Nels Tessem drove frantically toward the New Florence. They managed to park within a block of the place and had been there a few minutes when two of Capone's toughest-looking thugs walked up, eyed them, and sat themselves down on the front fenders of Frank's car. Frank started up the engine and drove around the corner to another spot just behind the restaurant. Immediately two more thugs appeared and did the same thing. Frank was finally forced to park outside the four-square-block area surrounding the place. It was one of Capone's cardinal rules that whenever he ventured from the Lexington, his hoodlums patrolled the four square blocks around the spot where he was going.

Inside the New Florence, Malone checked his gun and was led to a front table occupied by "Machine Gun" Jack McGurn and the notorious Paul "The Waiter" Ricca.

Capone's party was just getting under way, and it was lavish. The flower and chivalry of Chicago's thugdom—bookmakers, racketeers, bootleggers and triggermen—were all there, having a riotous time, laughing and shouting across the room at one another. They were all heavy drinkers, but they wouldn't think of drinking the stuff they themselves made or sold. Only the finest French champagnes and brandies were being consumed.

Malone, a nondrinker, sat watching them quietly.

He noticed that some of the food looked appetizing—flaming steaks and blood-rare sides of beef. It appeared to be a birthday party after all. A giant white cake had been installed in the center of the room, bearing the inscription "Happy Birthday Frank."

Capone himself, attired in tuxedo and black tie, circulated among the assembled guests, behaving like the perfect host, speaking to one and all in a most democratic manner. Finally he stopped just above Malone's shoulder. "Hiya," he smiled down.

"Hi, Al," Malone answered, beaming as loyally as possible.

Capone sauntered on. Malone felt himself suddenly breathe more easily.

At one stage of the festivities, an enormous steak was placed before Malone. He sliced off a piece, took a bite. His mouth began to burn—he swallowed—and instantly he felt a sizzling path spreading down from his throat to the pit of his stomach. His companions at the table eyed him blandly as he gasped for breath. He screamed for water. He was certain that he had been poisoned.

The waiter stood there a second, staring at him. "What the hell do you want water for, with all this champagne around?"

"Ulcers." Malone retched, gasping for air, gesturing helplessly.

The waiter finally relented, returning in a few moments with a pitcher of ice water. Malone rapidly gurgled down two full glasses, his stomach still on fire.

Slowly he began to feel relief. Perhaps he hadn't been poisoned after all.

"What's this?" Malone asked, elbowing Ricca, who was sitting next to him. He pointed to the steak.

[97]

"Spiced steak," replied Ricca. "Don't you like it?"

Malone lowered his head, trembling. To his horror he spotted a glint of metal plunging downward: during his convulsions his gun had been shaken loose from its belt holster. He sank over, feigning an attack of unbearable pain, and caught the gun just inches from the floor. He stayed bent over a second longer, pretending to be in total agony as he carefully slid the gun back up into its holster. Still holding his stomach, he shivered at the prospect that suddenly occurred to him—what would have happened if the gun had gone rattling across the floor?

He peeked out of the corner of his eye. Apparently Ricca hadn't spotted him sliding the gun back up into its holster.

At dawn Frank and Nels Tessem left the scene. They weren't sure whether Malone was alive or dead, but they knew there was nothing more they could do.

Frank arrived home, and within minutes his phone rang. It was Malone. He had overheard some things about Nitti at the party. One of them was a comment someone had made about Nitti's having some dealings with the Schiff Trust and Savings Bank.

Later that same morning Nels Tessem visited the Schiff Bank. To his inquiries the bank officials haughtily retorted that they had never heard of Frank Nitti. So Tessem, flashing a government subpoena, started checking the books and accounts. He found nothing in the deposit slips to indicate that Nitti banked there under his or any other name. He looked through the paying-teller's sheets, then the collection register. Finally he brusquely demanded to see the general ledger of the bank and the general-ledger tickets. There he found a long list of checks credited to Frank Nitti. Bank president Bruno Schiff finally admitted that he had entered into a secret agreement with Nitti to clear checks and deliver cash without showing the Enforcer's name on the records.

After a few more days of intense digging, Frank informed Irey, "I think we've got Nitti." Enough evidence had been gathered to support what looked like an indictment. Frank hurried the evidence to United States Attorney George E. Q. Johnson.

George E. Q. Johnson (he had adopted the "Q" to distinguish himself from the countless other George Johnsons) was a cool esthete with silken gray hair, parted straight as a ruler down the middle, curling at the edges. A dandified dresser who smoked long cylindrical cigars, he seemed little impressed by the sordid trial-life around him. He could be as intense and tough as Frank Wilson, but he preferred to let others do the dirty work. U.S. Attorney Johnson was astonished that so much evidence had been dug up. "Let's go," he told the investigators. "We'll get the grand jury without delay."

The Chicago newspapers followed up with banner headlines announcing Nitti's prospective indictment. In accordance with the usual procedure, a warrant for Nitti's arrest was issued and turned over to the United States marshal. But the marshal soon afterward reported to George Johnson that Nitti had disappeared.

U.S. Attorney Johnson was now on the spot. Even though it should have been the responsibility of the state's attorney's office, he went to Frank and begged him to find Nitti. "I know it's not your duty, but somebody's got to uphold the reputation of the government." The task had once again fallen to Frank and his agents to perform an out-of-the-ordinary act to carry on their investigation.

[99]

That morning Frank spread his men out in different directions to search for Nitti. Four exhausting days later, Frank reported to Irey:

We have been devoting considerable time in an attempt to locate Mr. Frank Nitti, and believe that he will be apprehended within a few days, unless something unexpected happens. Last week I communicated with Harlow, and arranged a meeting with Macey.* Macey furnished me with the Illinois license number of an auto being used by Nitti, and also informed me that Nitti at times uses a Ford automobile with a Wisconsin license. I then had Special Agent Malone** look for autos with the Illinois license number, or with a Wisconsin license.

Last Saturday afternoon he was in Berwyn, a suburb near Chicago, and he saw a car with the Illinois license number in which we were interested speeding up the street. The car was driven by a lady. He stopped a citizen in an auto,*** and persuaded the citizen to trail the auto in which we were interested. The lady visited several stores, and after two hours she returned to an apartment and entered it. We find, through the telephone company, that about six weeks ago a person using the name of Ralph Belmont had an unlisted phone installed in Apartment Three of the apartment the lady entered. We drove by the apartment several times on Saturday afternoon and Sunday, and saw the two autos described by Macey parked in front of it.

Staking out the premises, Agent Madden recalled, Frank "obtained permission to keep the apartment house under observation from the windows of a church diagonally across the street." There he stationed Special

---

* An underworld informer close to Nitti.
** Temporarily on leave from the Lexington Hotel.
*** A. P. Madden related that Malone in fact "leaped to the running board of an automobile, which followed closely. It happened that the driver of the second car was a mechanic who was out on a testing drive."

Agents Malone and Tessem as lookouts on an around-the-clock basis. Frank telegraphed Irey:

I feel reasonably certain we will have our man in custody within a few days. Considerable time has been spent on the Nitti angle, but believe has been spent to very good advantage if our plans are successful.

Just before midnight the following day, Mike Malone spotted an individual entering the apartment house who might have been Nitti, except that his hair was a different color and he had a thick moustache. Tessem and another agent hurried in after the man, accosting him in the hallway. The surprised suspect denied that he was Nitti, showing them his business card: Ralph Belmont, Sales Manager, Continental Co., 101 Wall Street, New York City.

The suspect was taken to the Cook County jail, where he was placed in a cell. Within minutes Frank arrived. The week before, he had located in a Cicero bank a personal checking account which he believed was Nitti's. Frank brought with him a twenty-five-dollar check which had been drawn on the account. It was made out to the Salvation Army.

"You're not such a bad guy," Frank said, grinning at the suspect through the bars. "You gave the Salvation Army twenty-five bucks last month."

"How in the hell did you know about that?" the suspect asked, nearly choking.

"Here's your canceled check covering that generous donation." Frank poked it in at him.

The suspect took a good look at the check and blurted out, "They came around every month begging for money, and I helped them out. That time I didn't have anything smaller than a grand in my pocket, so I gave them the check."

Within a week, Frank "The Enforcer" Nitti was in court. His bank account showed deposits of over $200,000 in six months. He admitted that the money was his cut from the profits of alcohol stills in Cicero, Little Sicily, and the West Side of Chicago, and from a Cicero gambling casino known as The Ship. Frank hastily began a memo to Elmer Irey:

Mr. Frank Nitti is now under indictment for failure to file tax returns 1926 to 27 and 28, also for evasion of income taxes. The amount of tax fixed by the Government against the defendant Nitti is————.

Frank left the figure blank. Proof had already been presented to the grand jury that Nitti had accumulated over $700,000 in 1925, 1926, and 1927 without paying any tax on it.

Faced with the evidence, Nitti pleaded guilty and was sentenced to one and a half years. A day later he was on his way to Leavenworth Penitentiary.

Frank cautiously explained the quick handling of Nitti's case to Irey. "Nitti got careless. Al hasn't."

In the weeks that followed, Frank went after other members of the Capone syndicate for tax evasion. "Greasy Thumb" Jack Guzik, Capone's financial manager, was indicted and sentenced to Leavenworth for five years. Ralph Capone, Al's brother, was given a three-year sentence. Sam "Big Belly" Guzik, the 350-pound brother of Jack, was also nailed for a three-year sentence.

Each time a conviction was secured, the press announced the news in big banner headlines. The citizens of Chicago were finally awakening from their fearful doze, pricked by the rumor that the government was moving to break the back of organized crime.

Frank decided it was time to close in on Capone.

8
EVIDENCE

The windowless cubicle the government had assigned to him in the old Federal Building was so cramped that Frank could barely move without barging into a filing cabinet or another agent. The temperature rose at times to over a hundred degrees. Frank complained of the cramped conditions to Irey:

We are now using four cabinets in this office, and we are badly in need of two or three more, as the old desk I am using cannot be locked, and the ancient flat top desk used by the other agents cannot be locked. I have tried to get the use of an additional steel cabinet, but they are needed for other purposes. I tried today to borrow a cabinet from the United States Attorney's Office, and they are "to let me know about it"; that is the usual stall around here. Plenty of encouragement that we will have additional space, etc., but no results. I do not have much hopes about space or filing cabinets. Perhaps you could send me three of the cabinets with locks. It takes several months to secure them in the ordinary course.

Could you secure authority for us to rent a suite of three offices in a private building? In that event we should have authority for a telephone. We also should have a stenographer, and furniture would have to be purchased. . . . I would not bother you about these matters if I could get assistance here, or if I could see the end of this work in sight, but I felt you would be interested. We cannot work effectively, efficiently, or intelligently under the present conditions, and it may affect our health or our good nature to work under these conditions during the summer months.

In a few days Frank received a note from Irey:

The Commissioner and I have both read, with a great deal of interest, your letter of March 27th with respect to the situation in the Al Capone case. The progress which you have made is remarkable and we are delighted with the prospects. I expect to see Mr. Youngquist* within the next day or two and shall be glad to show him your letter.

But no mention was made of renting a bigger office, although Irey did acknowledge:

We will take up with the supply division the question of getting you filing cabinets and desks.

Consequently, throughout the sweltering summer of 1930, Frank, in shirtsleeves and wringing wet, closeted himself in the tiny room, poring over mountains of paper, dating back as early as 1924, which had been seized by the police in raids on Capone's establishments. With his two assistants, William Hodgins and Nels Tessem, he combed the material a dozen times— close to two million separate items: bank records, faded old receipts, bits of paper with handwritten notations, anything that might furnish a shred of evidence linking Capone to the source of his profits.

* Assistant to the Attorney General of the United States.

[106]

Frank had no witnesses; most of those who could testify against Capone had fled or were too terrified to appear before a grand jury. Frank had promised protection for some of them, but they had laughed in his face. A second frustrating year was slowly dragging by. "We had leads," Frank admitted, "—some fairly good ones—but nothing big enough to make a case." In August, he wrote Irey:

Wish I could report some more definite accomplishments of our investigation. It is a slow job.

Regarding his fellow agents, he went on:

The continued hot weather has made them pretty tired, and as this case is apt to stretch out for two or three months longer it is the right thing for them to be given some leave during the summer. Agent Hodgins, who has been with me most of the time, is going to take leave the last two weeks of this month. The various memos, files, correspondence, exhibits, transcripts, and interviews gathered by us since we arrived in Chicago and also by Chicago special agents during the last years are voluminous.

One night, after a fruitless eighteen-hour day, Frank, after sending Hodgins and Tessem home, telephoned Judith from a pay phone to tell her he'd be late. Then he returned to the choking-hot little office and spread out everything—every bit of paper—to go over it all again.

The hours rolled on. By 1:00 in the morning, he was so bleary-eyed he couldn't see. Exhausted, the flesh on his back and arms clammy with sweat, he started gathering up the material piled all over the desk, the chairs, the floor, to return it to the filing cabinets. As he bent down to retrieve a bundle of checks, he accidentally bumped one of the file cabinet doors. It clicked closed, locking automatically.

He didn't have a key. His clumsiness filled him with sudden anger. As he grumbled to himself, discouraged, depressed, he began poking absentmindedly at the piles of paper strewn around the room.

Then he remembered the deserted storeroom just down the corridor.

He headed toward it, flicking on the light as he entered. The room was empty, except for one old filing cabinet. Managing to wrench open one of the drawers, he began clearing a space by removing the contents— several dusty bundles tied with string. Bunched up in back was a package covered in brown paper.

Something prompted him to examine the package. He snipped the string, and out fell three bound ledgers edged in red.

He thumbed through the first ledger but didn't see anything that made much sense. He started leafing through the second. Suddenly he stopped, electrified. Staring back at him was a page of columns headed: "Bird Cage," "21," "Craps," "Faro," "Roulette," "Horse bets."

He was no longer exhausted. Hurrying the ledger back to his desk, he sat down and began analyzing it, entry by entry. Here was the financial record of an enormous gambling operation. The neatly handwritten pages showed a take that ran from twenty to thirty thousand dollars a day. As his excitement grew, he riffled at random through the book. Every few pages a total balance had been entered, then divided among "A," "R," and "J." A balance totaled on December 2, 1924, was divided:

Town	$6,537.42	(paid)
Ralph	1,634.35	
Pete	1,634.35	
Frank	5,720.22	
J. & A.	5,720.22	
Lou	5,720.22	
D.	5,720.22	

But it was the notation at the top of one of the pages that instantly cleared his brain: "Frank paid $17,500 for Al."

There were more mentions of Al. Every month the heavy profits were divided—after the biggest share had been set aside for "Town." "Town," Frank knew, was a gangland term for graft paid to city officials.

Here was evidence of profits. But to make it mean anything to twelve jurors, Frank knew that there would have to be proof that the cryptic "Al" meant Capone.

By 9:00 that morning Frank had laid out the ledger before the staff of the state's attorney's office. There it was quickly identified as having been among the papers seized in the vigilante raid on the Hawthorne Smoke Shop *following William McSwiggin's murder on April 26, 1926.*

Like a far-off echo, the words of Police Sergeant Anthony McSwiggin came to mind: "I'll never rest until I've killed my boy's slayers or seen them hanged. That's all I have to live for now." After five years, McSwiggin's agonized pledge now loomed like a dark shadow over the career of his son's unconvicted killer.

Frank furnished himself with the names of the individuals who had taken part in the raid on the Hawthorne Inn, and set out to interview each of them personally.

One of the first men he interviewed was Chester H. Bragg, a real estate operator. Bragg recalled that during the commotion, Capone had appeared in his pajama tops, ruffled and unshaven. Obviously awakened by the crowd, Capone had raced across the street from the hotel in which he was living and tried to halt the raiders. "I'm the owner of this place!" he wailed, stumbling toward the closed door of the premises. At this point, another vigilante, David H. Morgan, chided the fat, comic-looking, pajama-clad mobster: "What do you think this is, a party?"

Capone roared back at him, "It ought to be my party! I *own* this place!"

Capone was not arrested during the raid. But this hardly assuaged his anger, and he took out his fury on Bragg and Morgan. Gravel was inserted in the cylinders and pistons of Bragg's new automobile, ruining it forever. Morgan was less fortunate. One night, a month later, he was accosted by three of Capone's thugs, who shot him and left him to die.

Both Bragg and Morgan, fearing for their lives, had tried to live obscurely since the raid. But they now promised to testify if needed. Frank took sworn testimony from each of them. The following is the interview with Chester H. Bragg, recorded by stenographer Marie J. Donahue in the Federal Building in Chicago:

Memorandum of interview held in Room 587 Federal Building, Chicago, Illinois, with Mr. Chester H. Bragg, 3101 Harlem Avenue, Berwyn, Illinois, in the presence of Special Agent Frank J. Wilson.

    Q. What is your full name?
    A. Chester H. Bragg.
    Q. What is your address?
    A. 3101 Harlem Avenue, Berwyn, Illinois.
    Q. What is your business?
    A. Real estate broker.

Evidence

Q. Will you kindly state the circumstances and details with reference to a raid which was conducted at a gambling establishment in Cicero, Illinois, on Kentucky Derby Day, 1926, at 4818 West 22nd Street?

A. I was called up the day previous by Reverend H. C. Hoover,* who asked me if I would report at eleven o'clock the following day at this Grove Avenue place where Morgan lived, number 3545, for some investigation. I came there at that time and met a squad car with about three state's attorney sheriffs, and we discussed plans, and landed up at 4818 22nd Street, Cicero, just before the noon hour, probably 11:45. Hoover and one other investigator had been there an hour in this gambling place, playing the games and getting the low-down on their activities. When we arrived, the place was put under arrest, and everybody, including our operators, were lined up against the wall (I mean Hoover and this other party). I was stationed as guard at the front entrance and told to let nobody out or in. There was a crowd congregated in the street that rapidly reached three or four thousand people. The noon-hour crowd at the Western Electric was then filling the streets, and the people from the Western Hotel (at that time it was called Anton's Hotel**) across the street soon learned about this, including Al Capone, who came across to the front door and tried several times to get in there. I stayed there and held the door, but he tried to push it open three or four times. I closed it each time. Finally he made a desperate effort to get the door open, and I opened it part way, and then I discovered from his scarred face who he was. I knew from pictures and other information I had. He said, "Let me in, I am the owner of the place," and I greeted him, and said, "Come on in, Al, we are looking for you." He went on upstairs, where our party was dismantling and loading gambling equipment and bringing it down to the street to be loaded into trucks, and we had backed up to the front of this entrance. I think we also had a truck at the rear, thinking that we might load each way. I am not sure whether they brought much of that out the back way, or

---

* The leader of the vigilante raid on the Hawthorne Smoke Shop.
** Named after Anton the Greek, whom Capone had murdered in 1926.

[111]

whether it all came out the front. We loaded two or three truckloads full of wheels and all sorts of gambling equipment. When this job was finished, I went out of the front door with Morgan, a paid investigator, and the crowd milled around so, trying to get at us, and knock us down. They followed us all the way across the street, and as I was trying to get into my car, I was slugged and my nose was broken. Morgan also was knocked down, and they tried to kick his face in, and I got him on his feet, and the two of us made a run for our car, and I got in there with blood spouting from my face and nose, all over the windshield, wheel, and my clothes. We drove through to La Grange and conveyed these loads of gambling equipment, and they were locked in the La Grange police station for safekeeping. This evidence was used in a trial before Judge Dreher of Brookfield, and although this evidence was brought into the case, it was dismissed for lack of evidence.

Q. Were any threats of any nature conveyed to you on account of your activity with reference to this raid?

A. I was told by several foreigners, at different times, who leaned into my car, and made verbal threats to me, that they would get me if I didn't stay out of those activities. My Nash car was ruined by gravel thrown in on top of the cylinders and pistons, by somebody who was evidently trying to intimidate me. I was told through political connections in the town of Cicero that if I didn't watch my step it would be just too bad.

Q. During the raid that occurred at 4818 West 22nd Street, was it evident that Mr. Al Capone was the owner of the place by any other circumstance or action, other than his statement to you that he was the owner of the place?

A. His orders to the employees and the people in the place, and their recognition of his authority, were evidence to anybody that he was.

Q. Did you see or hear him issue orders to employees in that place at the time?

A. Understand that we had the place under arrest, and that all these fellows were lined up so that he couldn't give orders in the sense of telling them to do something that we wouldn't permit them to do, but I recall very distinctly that his authority was evidenced there by his conversation and the conversation of workers and people who were running the gambling joint.

Q. Then the actions of Mr. Capone and the actions of employees in the gambling establishment which you observed during the raid made it quite evident that they regarded Mr. Capone as the proprietor of the place?

A. Absolutely.

Frank forwarded the recorded interview with Bragg and Morgan to Elmer Irey with the comments:

I am enclosing a copy of a statement made by Chester A. Bragg, prominent real estate dealer in Cicero, in which he states that Al Capone admitted to him that he was the owner of this establishment. I am enclosing a copy of a report made by David H. Morgan, Investigator for the West Suburban Ministers and Citizens Association of Cicero and Berwyn, relating to a raid made by him and others on this gambling establishment, May 18, 1926. He states that during the raid he turned over to Lieutenant Davidson, the sheriff in charge of the raid, Mr. Al Capone, as the owner of the place, and I asked Morgan how he knew Al was the owner, and he stated that Al came to the place a few minutes after the establishment had been entered by the officers. The officers had placed a guard at the door with instructions not to allow anyone to enter. Al demanded that he be let in and told Mr. Morgan, "I am the owner of this place." When Al entered the establishment during the raid, he also said to Morgan and others, "This is the last raid you will ever pull." It was the last raid Morgan ever pulled. Morgan and Bragg were knocked down and assaulted by the gang that afternoon when they left the gambling establishment. A month later three men were waiting in an alley near Morgan's garage when he returned home about midnight. They apparently were going to take him for "a ride," as they were armed and demanded him to accompany them. He resisted, and they shot him, leaving him to die, but he was not fatally wounded and recovered in a month. He said he decided the raiding business was not healthy and that Al Capone had made good his threat that it would be the last raid he would ever make.

Frank realized that, by themselves, Capone's verbal admissions of ownership meant little—Capone would later deny ever having made the remarks. But if the bookkeeper whose handwriting appeared in the ledger could be located, his testimony, combined with that of Bragg and Morgan, might prove irrefutably that Capone was the owner.

Concerning the ledger itself, which Frank felt could be the key to the case, he wrote Irey:

On the night of April 26, 1926, Assistant State's Attorney for Cook County W. H. McSwiggin was murdered in Cicero, Illinois. Mr. McSwiggin had a few months before interviewed witnesses in a murder case in which Capone was alleged to be involved. Al Capone was accused of the McSwiggin murder, and the police raided his Cicero gambling establishment on that date. This book was found in the safe of the establishment by the police during the raid, and it was turned over at that time to Special Agent P. F. Roche of the Chicago Division. As no tax case was pending against Capone, no use was made of this book, and it was filed in the Chicago office. After this investigation had proceeded for several months, during which time a careful search was made in Chicago, Cicero and other cities for records relating to the income of the Capone organization, this book was accidentally discovered by the writer in a miscellaneous lot of apparently unimportant papers left by Mr. Roche when he resigned from the government service. The book had no identification marks upon it, and its value as evidence relating to the income of Alphonse Capone had not been realized.

9
THE WITNESS

The handwriting in the ledger was neat, almost flowery. The capital letters that began each word were cleanly separated from the lower-case letters that followed. The figures were carefully jotted and were added in columns with black ink. There were no errors.

Frank guessed that the man he was looking for was a bookkeeper by trade—someone who was aware of how the gambling profits were parceled out, but who could be counted on to keep his mouth shut.

Joined by agents Hodgins, Tessem and Converse, Frank began collecting handwriting samples of every known hoodlum in Chicago. Voting registers were checked, as well as savings accounts, police court records, bail bond certificates. Frank's tiny office filled with more mountains of paper. The process went on for weeks. Frank wrote to Elmer Irey:

The Capone investigation is going steadily ahead. Not as fast as I would like to have it, but the evidence in the case against Al has been strengthened since my last letter to you.

[115]

Finally, one afternoon a deposit slip turned up from a little bank in Cicero. The signer was a Leslie Adelbert Shumway. The handwriting was identical with that in the ledger.

Frank learned from an underworld source: "Shumway is a perfect little gentleman, refined, slight, harmless—not like a racketeer at all."

But Shumway was nowhere to be found. Coroner's reports were checked; police records were searched thoroughly. Suspecting that Shumway might have followed the Capone gang to Florida to work in a gambling joint or at one of the race tracks, Frank traveled to Miami. He checked into a hotel there under a fictitious name and headed for the Hialeah race track. It was a hot, sunny day when he took his place at the rail. As he had a fair description of Shumway, he began studying the faces in the stands behind him. His gaze finally settled on the box seat section. Suddenly he found himself staring directly into the face of the man he had been stalking for two years—sitting with a bejeweled mistress on either side of him, smoking a long Havana cigar, occasionally raising his binoculars to his eyes, then lowering them to beckon one of a parade of fawning sycophants who waited to shake his hand. The image filled Frank with sudden disgust. "I looked upon his pudgy olive face, his thick pursed lips, the rolls of fat descending from his chin—and the scar, like a heavy pencil line across his left check—and clenched my lips in frustration. 'Good God,' I thought, 'when a country cop wants a man he just walks up and says, *You're pinched*. Here I am, with the whole United States Government behind me, as powerless as a canary!'"

Turning his back on Capone, who was puffing away on his seventy-five-cent Havana cigar, Frank bit off the end of one of his own nickel stogies and continued studying the faces of the crowd. But he did not locate Shumway at Hialeah.

That night Frank received an urgent call summoning him back to Chicago.

Capone had retained a high-salaried Washington tax attorney, Lawrence Mattingly, who had let the Intelligence Unit know that Capone wished to clear up any indebtedness to the government. On his way back to Chicago, Frank fired off a memo to Elmer Irey:

. . . it may be advisable to talk to the taxpayer at Washington instead of at Chicago. If, in the meantime, his attorney Mattingly calls at your office regarding the case, you might suggest to him that it may be advisable at a later date to have him produce the taxpayer at Washington and if possible let Mattingly get the idea that the suggestion regarding the Washington conference comes from the Bureau at Washington, *not* from Chicago.

But upon Frank's arrival, Mattingly telephoned to let him know that his client was ready to furnish all information about his business activities.

"Bring him in," Frank quickly responded. "I want to talk to him."

Al Capone presented himself at Room 587 of the Federal Building in Chicago a few days later, leaving a cordon of well-armed bodyguards stationed just outside. The affair had the appearance of a warring general coming to discuss terms of peace. Present with Frank to meet Capone were Ralph Herrick, the tax agent in charge of the Chicago enforcement unit; Special Agent William Hodgins, and a stenographer, Winnifred M. Kinnebrew.

Mattingly performed the introductions. "This is my client, Mr. Alphonse James Capone."

Frank had never met Capone. He noted that the

gangleader "was about six feet tall, 240 pounds, powerful shoulders and arms, shifty dark eyes, a fine set of white teeth and a protruding stomach. The vicious-looking scar on the left side of his face extended for about six inches. He was dressed immaculately in a stylish dark blue double-breasted suit with a neat white linen handkerchief, its four sharp points protruding about one inch from the upper pocket. He wore a ring set with a big diamond, and a heavy gold-and-diamond-studded watch chain, which he fingered nervously. He had on black sport shoes with white tips, blue silk socks with white clocks, and a snappy blue necktie with large white polka dots. He had a big flabby paw and dainty manicured nails. When he pulled out a silk handkerchief, I got a strong whiff of lily-of-the-valley."

Agent Ralph Herrick began the interrogation. "I think it is only fair to say that any statements which are made here, which could be used against you, probably would be used."

"Insofar as Mr. Capone can answer any questions without admitting his liability to criminal action," Mattingly countered, "he is here to cooperate with you and work with you."

Herrick directed the first question to Capone. "What records have you of your income, Mr. Capone—do you keep any records?" Capone kept his reply low and respectful. "No, I never did." "Any checking accounts?" "No, sir." "How long, Mr. Capone, have you enjoyed a large income?" "I never had much of an income." "I will state it a little differently—an income that might be taxable." "I would rather let my lawyer answer that question." Mattingly hurriedly cut in. "Well, I'll tell you. Prior to 1926, John Torrio, who happens to be a client of mine, was the employer of Mr. Capone, and up to that point it is my impression that Mr. Capone's income wasn't there. He was in the position of an employee, pure and simple. That is the information I get from Mr. Torrio and Mr. Capone."

At that moment, Frank took over the questioning. He remembered that "Scarface's sullen smile turned to an angry scowl."

WILSON: Have you ever filed income tax returns?

CAPONE: No.

WILSON: What was your marital status during the years under question—were you married?

CAPONE: Absolutely.

WILSON: Any children?

CAPONE: Yes, one.

WILSON: How old?

CAPONE: Twelve.

WILSON: For the years mentioned, did you buy or sell any real estate?

CAPONE: No, sir.

WILSON : Did you furnish any money to purchase real estate which was placed in the name of others?

CAPONE: I would rather let my lawyer answer that question.

MATTINGLY: I have no objection to answering that question. Mr. Capone bought a piece of property in Miami, Florida, in the name of his wife in the year 1928.

WILSON: Did you furnish the money to pay for that property?

CAPONE: Yes.

WILSON: What was the purchase price of that property?

CAPONE: $10,000 cash, $30,000 mortgage.

WILSON: What was the source of the money you used to make your cash payment?

CAPONE: I would rather let my lawyer answer that question.

[119]

Mattingly objected.

At that moment, Frank remembered, Capone became noticeably disturbed. "He stalled, evaded direct answers, and never looked me straight in the eye."

WILSON: Did you purchase any securities during the years under consideration?

CAPONE: No, I never had anything like that.

WILSON: Did you have any brokerage accounts in your own name?

CAPONE: No.

WILSON: Did you have any brokerage accounts under an assumed name?

CAPONE: No.

WILSON: Did your wife or relatives have any brokerage accounts, or did they purchase any securities?

CAPONE: I would rather not answer that question.

WILSON: Are you interested in any way in the Roosevelt Securities Company?

CAPONE: No.

WILSON: Roosevelt Finance Company?

CAPONE: No.

WILSON: Do you care to give us any statement of your assets and liabilities at the present time?

CAPONE: My lawyer is taking care of all that.

WILSON: Have you any record of the monies which you might have spent for expenses during the four years under review?

CAPONE: No. I have no records whatsoever.

WILSON: You employed several attorneys during the four years under review—have you any idea as to the fees you paid them?

CAPONE: I would rather let my lawyer answer that question.

WILSON: Were your financial transactions, particularly disbursements, usually handled in currency?

CAPONE: Yes.

WILSON: You have no canceled checks or check stubs?

CAPONE: No.

[120]

Frank Wilson—The man who got Capone.

St. Valentine's Day Massacre. *United Press International*

Fred "Killer" Burke, the man who pulled the trigger at the St. Valentine's Day Massacre. *United Press International*

Capone on his Palm Island estate.
New York Daily News

Chicago Mayor William Hale "Big Bill" Thompson, who popularized the expression, "Vote early and vote often."
Wide World Photos

"Machine Gun" Jack McGurn, Capone's dapper triggerman. *United Press International*

The courtroom in the Federal Building in Chicago. *International Newsreel*

(*At left*) U.S. Attorney George E. Q. Johnson. *United Press International*

A confident Capone chats with attorneys Michael Ahern and Albert Fink on the first day of his trial. *Wide World Photos*

U.S. Federal Judge James H. Wilkerson. *United Press International*

Pete Penovich, former manager of the Hawthorne Smoke Shop, leaving the Grand Jury chambers, where he has just testified (after being primed by the mob) that the ledger notation, "Frank paid $17,500 for Al," represented credit to Capone for a horse bet. *United Press International*

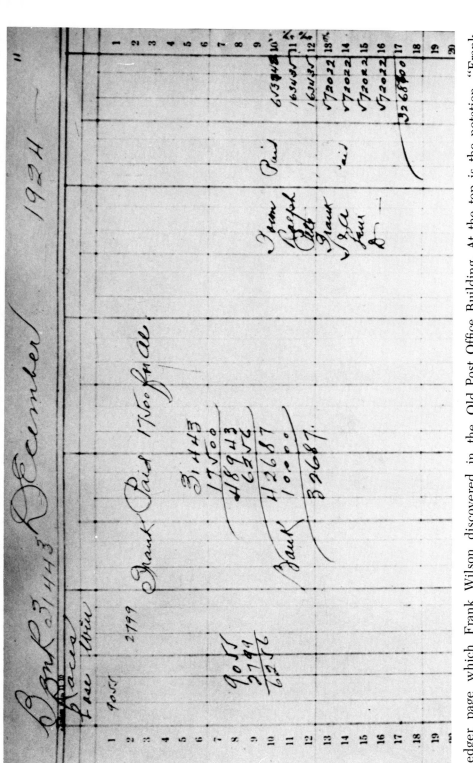

Ledger page which Frank Wilson discovered in the Old Post Office Building. At the top is the notation, "Frank paid $17,500 for Al."

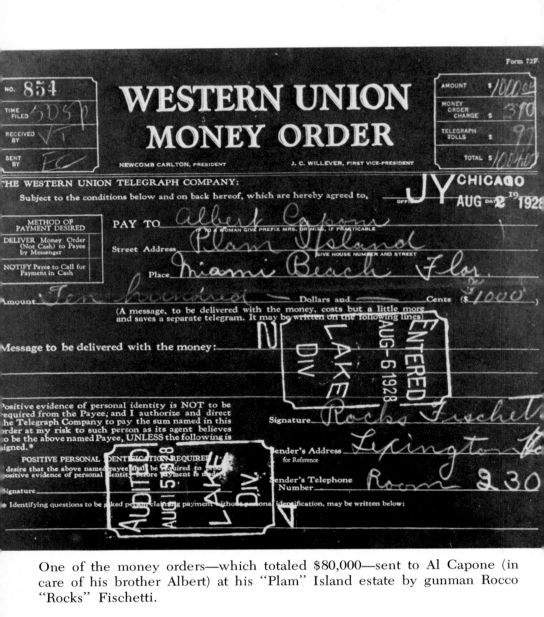

One of the money orders—which totaled $80,000—sent to Al Capone (in care of his brother Albert) at his "Plam" Island estate by gunman Rocco "Rocks" Fischetti.

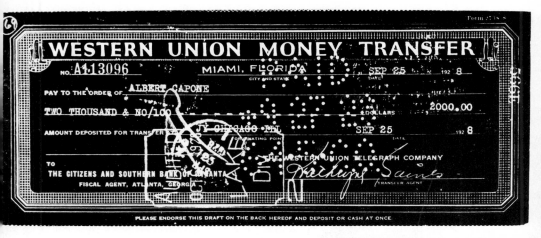

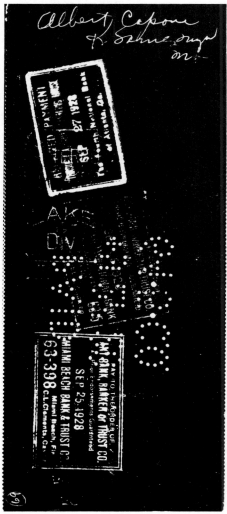

Another sample of part of the $80,000 identified by Parker Henderson, made out to Albert Capone but endorsed and cashed by Alphonse.

Johnny Torrio (*wearing hat*), Capone's first and only partner. *Wide World Photos*

(*At left*) Jake "Greasy Thumb" Guzik, Capone's business manager. *Wide World Photos*

Stunned, Capone leaves the Federal courtroom after being sentenced to eleven years by Judge James H. Wilkerson. Over Capone's left shoulder is the face of Special Agent Michael Malone (*in white hat*), watching Capone. Moments later Malone joined Capone on the freight elevator which took Capone to the basement. *Wide World Photos*

WILSON: What did you do with your money—carry it on your person?

CAPONE: Carried it on my person.

MATTINGLY: After Mr. Capone leaves and this interview is over, I should like to discuss this matter with you gentlemen, probably make some arrangement suitable to your convenience.

HERRICK: I know you spoke of going to Florida or somewhere. Then you mean you can start this morning, taking this matter up?

MATTINGLY: Yes. I should like to spend Easter with my family in Florida, and I had thought, gentlemen, that it might be possible to postpone this until next week, but that is a matter for you to decide.

HERRICK: It is a matter that we all want cleaned up, and, if possible, I think it would be desirable to make a start on it. If we have to defer it later, there isn't any disposition on our part to keep you away from your family over Easter, but it seems to me that the quicker we get started on it, the better it will be.

After the stenographer had been dismissed, Capone pulled out a fistful of Corona cigars and offered Frank one. "I don't smoke," Frank retorted, then hammered back at him, "Were you ever connected with the Hawthorne Dog Track?"

Capone sizzled. "I would rather not answer that question."

With that, Frank let him have it. Did his wife or relatives keep safe-deposit boxes? What about the money wired to him in Florida?

Capone's eyes narrowed. "Somebody's trying to push me around." He stared icily at Frank. "How's your wife, Wilson?" Getting up to leave, he remarked pointedly, "You be sure to take care of yourself."

Capone left the room. There was dead silence.

"Frank," warned Hodgins, "watch your step from now on."

10
OWNERSHIP

On September 20, 1930, Capone's attorney, Lawrence Mattingly, submitted the following statement to the Internal Revenue:

Re: Alphonse Capone

The following statement is made without prejudice to the rights of the above named taxpayer in any proceedings that may be instituted against him. The facts stated are upon information and belief only.

The taxpayer is now 31 years old, and has continually lived with his wife since his marriage in 1917. He has one child, a son, now nearly 12 years old. Since 1922 he has been the principal support of his widowed mother and his sister and brother, now 19 and 21 years of age, respectively.

Prior to the latter part of the year 1925 he was employed at a salary which at no time exceeded $75.00 per week. During the years 1926 to 1929 inclusive, he was the recipient of considerable sums of money, title to which vested in him by right of possession only.

Taxpayer became active and a principal with three associates at about the end of the year 1925. Because of the fact that he had no capital to invest in their various undertakings,

[123]

his participation during the entire year 1926 and a greater part of the year 1927 was limited. During the years 1928 and 1929, the profits of the organization of which he was a member were divided as follows: one-third to a group of regular employees and one-sixth each to the taxpayer and three associates. The taxpayer was at no time the banker for the organization, nor did he ever actively participate in the conduct of its individual enterprises.

The only attorneys employed by the taxpayer personally during this period were Nash and Ahern, Ron Epstein and Captain Billy Waugh, all of Chicago, Illinois. The so called bodyguards with which he is reputed to surround himself on the occasion of infrequent appearances in public were not, as a general rule, his personal employees, but were, in fact, employees of the organization who participated in its profits. Several of these employees stopped at the same hotel with the taxpayer while he was in Chicago. That a large force of bodyguards did not continually surround him is established by the fact that on the occasion of his arrest in Philadelphia 1929, only one companion was with him.

The furniture in the home occupied by the taxpayer while he was in Florida was acquired at a cost not in excess of $20,000. The house and grounds have been thoroughly appraised, and the appraisal has heretofore been submitted to you. There is a mortgage against the house and grounds of $30,000. His indebetedness to his associates has rarely ever been less than $75,000 since 1927. It has frequently been much more.

Notwithstanding that two of the taxpayer's associates from whom I have sought information with respect of the amount of the taxpayer's income insist that his income never exceeded $50,000 in any one year, I am of the opinion that his taxable income for the years 1926 and 1927 might be fairly fixed and not to exceed $26,000 and $40,000, respectively, and for the years 1928 and 1929, not to exceed $100,000 per year.

Respectfully submitted,

Lawrence P. Mattingly,

Attorney-in-fact, for Alphonse Capone

By submitting such a letter, Mattingly had made a serious tactical blunder. The amounts didn't matter— Capone spent more than $100,000 a year on high living alone. But what he had turned over to the government was a *written admission* of Capone's tax delinquency.

By framing the document around the conditions stated in the first paragraph that it was made "without prejudice to the rights of the taxpayer in any proceedings that might be instituted against him," Mattingly had miscalculated. Such a stipulation was not legally binding.

Frank headed back to Florida. In a memo to Irey, he reported:

At the interview Capone was warned that anything he said would be used against him. He declined to answer some questions, stating that he would prefer to have his lawyer answer for him. The letter of September 20th was submitted by Mattingly after he had stated to me several times that he would do his best to submit figures to the Bureau regarding the income of the taxpayer. I encouraged Mattingly to submit what he could to us and advised that what he submitted to help us to determine the tax liability of his client would receive serious consideration. . . . I was very anxious to get the taxpayer on record, and I also felt that we probably could capitalize and use to good advantage any figures submitted by Mattingly.

When we first read the letter of September 20th, we accepted the first paragraph in it at its face value, and considered that the letter could *not* be used against him in a criminal prosecution. After several discussions with attorney Green of the General Counsel's Office and attorneys Froelich and Clawson of the United States Attorney's office, they now tell me that it will be possible to use the letter in a criminal prosecution. If so, it will be of considerable help to us. . . .

The letter confirms the existence of a partnership or organization, and states that Al received one-third of the profits

[125]

of the organization during certain years. We can show Al Capone hiding his financial transactions by receiving money by Western Union wire, in Florida, under an assumed name.

Hundreds of these Western Union wires had already been collected by agents Tessem and Converse, substantiating that monies had been forwarded to members of Capone's family on a regular basis by certain of Capone's henchmen in Chicago, primarily Rocco "Rocks" Fischetti.

Summing up this aspect of the case, Frank wrote to Irey:

We have just completed an examination of all Western Union wire transfers from Chicago for 1927 and 1928 and located about $100,000 sent to members of Capone family or employees on the Capone estate at Palm Island, Miami Beach, Fla., by members of the Capone organization. This was a slow, tedious job, as about 500,000 checks were handled.

We believe these wire transfers can be introduced in evidence and that this will strengthen our case. Parker Henderson* has identified several of them, about $25,000 which he states he turned over to Al Capone. . . .

Rocco Fischetti, Charlie Fischetti, and Johnny Capone and other gangsters are senders of many of these wire transfers, and we are having trouble locating them. However, we will keep on looking and hope to get them. I am informed by my friend** that some of them are in the East, probably in New York. . . .

In the last two weeks we have formed additional evidence to establish the extravagant living of the taxpayer and witnesses to testify that he had an elaborate *office* in the Metropole hotel and Lexington hotel. The attorneys feel that these

---

* The son of the former mayor of Miami, a confidant of Capone, who loved to shoot dice and craps with him. Capone had presented him with a diamond-studded belt buckle.
** Eddie O'Hare.

[126]

witnesses will strengthen the case considerably and will be admitted as evidence. We found a lot of miscl. jewelry at one place for $5,000; 20 diamond belt buckles and miscellaneous items from another jeweler for about $10,000; hotel bills amounting to $20,000, furniture about $20,000; fourteen suits of clothes at $135.00 each from Marshall Field and Company in a period of three months in 1927. . . .

Proceeding in his hunt for the witness Leslie "Lou" Shumway, Frank continued hanging around the various race tracks and dog tracks in the Miami area. Realizing that it wouldn't be wise to start asking around for Shumway, he roamed from track to track, hoping to spot the "perfect little gentleman, refined, slight, harmless," who did not look like a racketeer at all.

One evening he ventured to a spot known as the Biscayne Bay Kennel Club. It was a wet, rainy night. Frank huddled under the grandstand, mingling with the crowd. Suddenly, way back behind the betting windows, in the cashier's department, he caught a glimpse of a man who matched Shumway's description.

Frank tailed the suspect after the races had ended for the day, and eventually saw him disappear into a one-family house in the suburban section of Miami.

The following morning Frank walked in on the suspect while he was having breakfast with his wife. Frank identified himself, and the suspect tremblingly blurted out that his name was Shumway. Frank invited him to his office in the Federal Building for a chat concerning a case he was working on, but refused to elaborate on the details of the case.

Shumway sat in stunned silence as Frank drove him over the Miami Causeway toward the Federal Building. Frank purposely refrained from naming the case or telling Shumway anything about it.

The Man Who Got Capone

Inside the Federal Building, Frank led Shumway into a private office and shut the door. "I am investigating the income tax liability of Alphonse Capone."

Shumway turned white; his hands suddenly quivered, his jaw began to rattle. Frank handed him a glass of water. "I've got something stronger across the hall if you'd like a shot, Lou."

With a swig or two of whiskey, Shumway managed to pull himself together. "Oh, you're mistaken, Mr. Wilson. I don't know Al Capone."

Frank put his hand on Shumway's shoulder. "Lou—I know you're in a helluva spot. You have two choices. If you refuse to play ball with me, I'll have to send a deputy marshal looking for you at the dog track. I'll have him ask for you by name and serve a subpoena on you. As soon as the gang knows the government has located you, they will pass the word to Scarface. Knowing your reputation as a gentleman and a truthful man, Scarface will probably decide to have you bumped off at once so you can't testify."

Frank hesitated. With a smile he added, "If you don't like that idea, Lou, take choice number two. Come clean with the United States Government and tell me the truth about this cash book and this ledger. You were bookkeeper at the Hawthorne Smoke Shop. You can identify every entry in these books—and you can tell who your boss was. I'll guarantee to keep it secret until the day of the trial. I'll send you away to a safe place where the Mafia can't locate you. You'll be guarded day and night. Play ball, Lou, and I'll guarantee that Mrs. Shumway will not become a widow."

Shumway's tortured face stared up at Frank. Finally, after another hour of trembling, he agreed to give the following statement:

[128]

Ownership

State of Florida)
) ss.
County of Dade)

Mr. Leslie A. Shumway, of Miami Beach, Florida, being duly sworn, deposes and says:

From about June of 1924 until May of 1926 I was employed in Cicero, Illinois, in a gambling establishment. On account of the illegal nature of this business, it was necessary to move from place to place in order to conduct the business without interference from law officers. The business was first conducted at No. 4848 West 22nd Street in a ground floor store in the Anton Hotel. A cigar store was operated in the front of the store by "Knock-out" Brown, and the rest of the store was used for the gambling business. This business consisted of taking bets on horse races, roulette wheel, craps, twenty-one game and poker. There were approximately from 40 to 50 persons employed in the business. The business at times was moved to 4838, 4835 and 4818 West 22nd Street, the Subway and upstairs over the Subway. All of these various places were in Cicero, Illinois. The business was conducted by the same employees and the same owner at each of these places. In addition to the business conducted at these places, the business also conducted a book on the horse races at the Hawthorne Race Track.

When I first started to work in this business I was hired by Frank Pope, who was manager of the horse race branch of the business. Pete Penovich was manager of that part of the business relating to games of chance, such as roulette, twenty-one, craps, poker and so forth. Orders and directions relating to my work in this business were issued to me by Frank Pope and Pete Penovich, whom I recognized as my superiors, and the only other person whom I recognized as an owner of the business and from whom I took orders relating to the business was Mr. Alphonse Capone.

On one occasion I was present in our gambling establishment when a raid was made on the place by law officers who were accompanied by a minister, Rev. Mr. Hoover. The raid took place about noon and I was in charge of the establishment, as Frank Pope and Pete Penovich had not yet reported

[129]

for business. I was in the office and the raiding officers entered the office. The raiding officers were going to take possession of the bank roll or currency which we had on hand to do business with.

Mr. Alphonse Capone then appeared dressed in his pajama pants and coat. He objected to the officers taking the currency on hand and directed me to take possession of the cash. I carried out his instructions because I recognized and regarded him as one of the owners of the business.

Mr. Al Capone came into the establishment on frequent occasions. He did not stay in the part of the establishment where the patrons conducted their business, but he came to the office and talked with Frank Pope and Pete Penovich, the active managers of the business. At times he personally made bets with the establishment and was extended credit.

Shortly after I was first employed in this business, I was present one evening when some men whom I believed to be the owners of the business were in the office. They were Mr. Louis Elteria, Dion O'Banion, Louis La Cava, John Torrio and Alphonse Capone. Mr. Pete Penovich and Frank Pope were also present that evening. As the men mentioned desired to discuss some confidential matters relating to the business, I was requested by Pete Penovich to leave the office, which I did.

Some of the employees at the establishment were Frank Miliano, Frank McCreevy, Rogers, George Beer, Jimmy Stanton, Joe Faulkner.

During most of the time I was employed in this business, it was my duty to keep a daily record of the establishment in a cloth-bound book. One page of this book was used to cover the business for each month, and I made daily entries in this book showing the daily net profit or net loss from the races, the wheel, twenty-one game, poker, craps and so forth. I arrived at the entries entered in this book from written memorandums furnished to me daily showing the net gain or net loss from each branch of the business for the day. The salaries and other expenses of the business were deducted from the day's receipts each day, and the entry entered by me in the book record was the net profit or net loss of each branch of the business. I also checked the cash on hand each day in order to verify my book records with the currency on hand for the bankroll. On a very few occasions the cash did not exactly balance, but the difference was a very small amount.

I have today been shown a cloth bound book containing records of the business from May 1, 1924, to April 30, 1926, and I can definitely state that this is the book containing the records which I kept relating to the gambling business in Cicero which I have referred to in this affidavit. I have also been shown photostats of the monthly sheets in this book, upon which sheets I made the entries, and for the purpose of identification I have written my name on the reverse side of these sheets. The sheets upon which I made the entries in this book include the months of January to December, 1925, and January, February, March and April of 1926. I did not make the entries on the sheets for the months of May to December, 1924, but I was directed by Mr. Pete Penovich to perform work upon these sheets and I did check them, as my individual check mark and footings which I recognize appear upon them.

All the daily entries on the monthly sheets in this book correctly reflect the net profits or net losses of this business conducted at various places mentioned above during the periods referred to. The profit or surplus cash was not distributed by me. I worked on a salary and did not, at any time, receive any percentage of the profits except a small percentage I got on a pan game.

During the summer of 1925, the business conducted a book on the horse races at the Hawthorne Race Track, and I assisted Frank Pope on that book at the Hawthorne track for two days. The profits from the book conducted at the race track in 1924 are reflected in the book record which was kept, but the profits from the betting at the Hawthorne Race Track in 1925 are not reflected in the book record which I kept. Frank Pope kept track of the profits or losses resulting from the race track book conducted at the Hawthorne track in 1925.

I have been shown a sheet in the cloth-bound book which I kept, which sheet is marked "Expenses June 1925." This sheet is in my writing and indicates that the monthly overhead for salaries, rent, lights, and outside men and similar expenses of all departments of the business amounted to $24,622 for that month. The expenses for each department or branch of the business were deducted daily from the gross receipts of each department or branch of the business, and the daily entry which I made in the book record is the net profit or net loss of each department or branch of the business.

Mr. Ben Pope was also employed by this business. I was sick from February 26 to March 4, 1926, and he made the daily entries in the book record during that period. Mr. Pete Penovich discontinued his connection with the business a few months before the business was closed, and after Penovich left, Frank Pope was the manager of the business. Mr. Frank Pope was assisted by his brother, Ben Pope, and by myself. Assistant State's Attorney McSwiggin was killed in the spring of 1926, and shortly after that I was informed by Frank Pope that the gambling business would have to be closed.

During the period I was employed by this gambling business, many bets were made by wire with book-makers in various cities. If our establishment lost, we would send a check to the out-of-town book-maker, and if we would win we would receive a check from the out-of-town book-maker. Many of the checks which we received were deposited to the credit of Frank Pope in the Pinkert State Bank, and many of the checks received were cashed by me at the Pinkert State Bank at Cicero. These checks would come to Frank Pope, and I was authorized by him to endorse his name on checks to be cashed or deposited. I have been shown certain deposit slips for the account of Frank Pope in the Pinkert State Bank which were written by me. These deposits represent the business of the gambling establishment. When our establishment lost the bets which we made with out-of-town book-makers, we sent them a check to cover the loss and the check was drawn on a bank account which was kept at the Pinkert State Bank in the name of Frank Pope.

The book record of the business in which I made the daily entries was kept in a cabinet, and the only persons who had access to this book or who made entries in it were Mr. Peter Penovich, Mr. Frank Pope and Mr. Ben Pope.

(*Signed*) Leslie Adelbert Shumway

Subscribed and sworn to before me this 18th day of February, 1931.

(Signed) Frank J. Wilson,
Special Agent, Bureau of Internal Revenue

That night Frank spirited Shumway to California. His intention was to hide him there, to keep him alive until the time of the trial.

He now had his key witness, but the next task that lay before him was to show that the income from the Hawthorne Smoke Shop had actually reached Capone. In addition to figures in books, actual currency had to be shown finding its way into Capone's pockets.

Arriving back in Chicago, Frank began a thorough check on all recorded money transactions in Cicero. After a few days of this, he unearthed evidence pointing to a certain "J. C. Dunbar" who had brought to the Pinkert State Bank in Cicero enough gunnysacks full of cash to buy $300,000 worth of cashier's checks.

Frank was about to begin searching for the mysterious "J. C. Dunbar" when his private phone rang and Eddie O'Hare's agitated voice blurted over the receiver, "I've got to see you!"

"Okay, the taproom on Wilson Avenue," Frank answered.

Arriving at the spot where they had agreed to meet, Frank found O'Hare waiting, red-faced and tense. "Frank, you've got to move right away—this afternoon, I mean. Scarface has four Mafia killers from Brooklyn in town to bump you off—he's put a price of twenty-five grand on your head. They know you and your wife are living in Room 307 at the Sheridan Plaza Hotel—they have the garage spotted where you keep your car—they have machine guns!"

11
"KILL WILSON"

Incredulous, Frank stared at O'Hare. It seemed preposterous that Capone would make such a desperate move. "Why?"

"Who knows? Maybe Capone figures if he gets you, there'll be nobody left with the guts to prosecute him."

Frank gazed fixedly at O'Hare. The blue eyes, the heavy eyelids, the dark brow, the same features that had seemed so alive as Eddie related his boy Butch's dream of getting into the U.S. Naval Academy, now reflected his agitation.

"What do the killers look like?"

Eddie O'Hare shook his head. "I never saw any of them before. All I know is they're riding around town in a car with New York license plates."

Frank pushed himself from the table and solemnly telephoned his office. The other agents were out, but he learned that Mike Malone had been frantically trying to reach him. Malone had left a pay phone number. Frank telephoned the number and listened as the agitated Malone heatedly reported that, while sitting in the lobby of the Hotel Lexington, he had overheard two of Capone's lieutenants discussing the Mafia contract that had been taken out on Frank's life. The Mafiosi had arrived in town that morning. They were already out in a blue Chevrolet sedan looking for Frank.

"That lousy son of a bitch," Frank muttered, slamming down the phone. He said goodbye to O'Hare and started for the Sheridan Plaza Hotel.

Now to confront Judith. Luckily she had made a wistful remark a few days before that she'd like to live at the Palmer House. On his way to the Sheridan Plaza, he swerved his car to the curb and hurriedly telephoned an acquaintance—the house detective at the Palmer House. He followed with a call to Judith. "I have a surprise for you. We're moving to the Palmer House—this afternoon. Pack the stuff."

Driving his DeSoto to within three blocks of the Sheridan Plaza, he parked it and hailed a taxi. The cab dropped him off on the front steps of the hotel; he tore through the lobby and into the elevator.

Judith was practically packed when he arrived. There was no time for explanations. Hustling her out the door, he said, "I've got to work in the office for several nights. We can have dinner together every night if I am at a Loop hotel near the office."

Judith stared at him, bewildered. With their suitcases under his arms, they headed down into the lobby. "I have to leave. Have to run over to Kansas City," he shouted to the deskman on duty as they dashed out the front door.

Flagging a taxi, he and Judith jumped in and rode the three blocks to where he had parked his DeSoto. Grabbing Judith by the arm, he paid the fare, then left her at the curb as he hurried down the sidewalk to an apartment house a few doors away, shouting back that a new agent had just moved in—he wanted to say hello. Frank faked ringing the doorbell, came out a few seconds later and announced that the new agent wasn't home.

Judith stared at him, still silent.

They got into his car and he started the engine. Together they sped toward Union Station. "A new man's coming in on the train. I think I'll meet him," Frank suddenly informed her. Parking the car directly in front of the terminal, he helped Judith, struggling with her bags, into the crowded station. By this time Judith was totally confused. Frank prayed that Capone's torpedoes were confused too.

As Frank clutched Judith's arm, they pushed their way into the bustling crowd—deeper toward the center of the station—up and down stairways, across ramps, cutting through to the rear platform—finally scurrying up the stairs and out, around the corner, across the bridge, down Adams Street, and into the lobby of the Palmer House.

He checked in and accompanied the startled Judith up to the room he had reserved on the top floor, leaving her there. He promised he would return in half an hour.

Charging back out into the street, he headed for the state's attorney's office at 54 West Austin Avenue. Within minutes he had sworn out a warrant for Al Capone's arrest.

Then, Frank and a dozen detectives under the supervision of State's Attorney's Chief Investigator Pat Roche tore out into the streets to look for the killers. All they had to go on was the description of the blue Chevrolet with New York license plates.

Within seconds, an informant working in the state's

attorney's office tipped off Capone. Capone listened to the news and reacted instantly, ordering the contract to be paid off and sending his henchmen out to halt the Mafiosi. Capone himself headed for the airport to hop a plane to Florida.

Frank never caught up with the blue Chevrolet. It disappeared from the city in the wee hours of the morning, its treacherous occupants returning to the back alleys of Brooklyn.

Despite the fact that the state's attorney's staff had been solemnly sworn to secrecy, the following morning the Chicago *Tribune* printed the entire story on its front page. The article related in detail how Capone had imported four Mafia killers to assassinate Frank J. Wilson, the head of the Intelligence Unit's Special Investigative Force. When Frank read the article he was infuriated.

I was much disgusted [he wrote Irey] when I read the story this morning about the public disclosure of the plans of Capone to bring four gunmen to Chicago from New York. . . . By that breach of confidence the lives of our informants* may be in jeopardy, and our chances of obtaining further help from this source may be eliminated.

Judith was with Special Agent James Sullivan's wife the following morning when the copy of the *Tribune* arrived. Alice Sullivan did her best to hide it, but just before noon Judith noticed the front-page article relating Capone's attempt to murder her husband.

Alice Sullivan telephoned Frank later at his office to tell him that Judith was sobbing hysterically. She urged him to hurry home.

"No," Frank replied quietly, "it's best she fight it out alone."

* O'Hare and Malone.

[138]

12
THE COP HATER

Judith ordered his favorite dinner sent up for Frank when he got back that evening—steak, baked potatoes, and a salad of fresh garden vegetables, topped off with his favorite dessert, an ice cream sundae covered with walnuts and strawberry syrup. Frank made no mention of the article in the newspaper. Neither did she.

They dined without a word. After dinner they went for a drive in the country. There, in the still darkness, in a quiet, controlled voice, Judith finally murmured, "Frank, I read about your assignment in the paper—I've been thinking about it all day—I know you wouldn't want to quit in the middle of a case—it wouldn't be fair to ask you. . . ." She hesitated a second, holding back her tears. "From now on, we just have to pray harder for your safety and harder for your success than we ever did before. But remember"—her voice suddenly grew fiery—"you have to promise to take me with you whenever you can, so I can help you!"

Frank gathered her in his arms, moved by the image that came to him. Judith—all of five feet; Judith, who

[139]

loved tiny, helpless things—babies, puppies, birds fallen from their nests—wanted to protect him from the Capone mob!

A Mafia contract was one of the more exotic methods used by Capone to intimidate, coerce or devastate his foes. But the terror of the simple "one-way ride" still hung heavily over the heads of the residents of Chicago. Capone's enforcers were everywhere. It was as if he now sensed that he was engaged in a life-and-death struggle, and with the instinct of a hunted animal, Capone began thrusting out his tentacles in all directions.

When agents Nels Tessem and William Hodgins arrived at the Pinkert State Bank in Cicero to check various transactions, the cashier replied that the bank would be happy to help. But when Hodgins asked certain pointed questions about the bank's transactions, direct or indirect, with the syndicate or its gambling establishments, the cashier flatly denied any such dealings.

Realizing that the employees of the bank had obviously been threatened, agents Tessem and Hodgins requested all canceled cashier's checks from the years 1926–1928. The cashier, at first reluctant, finally provided them with the checks. Examining them, Tessem and Hodgins discovered several that had been purchased by and made payable to the mysterious "J. C. Dunbar," usually in amounts of $10,000 or $20,000; together they totaled $450,000. In addition, half the canceled checks had been endorsed by Capone's financial aide, Jack Guzik.

Meanwhile, Frank had pinned down the identity of the nefarious J. C. Dunbar. With Eddie O'Hare's help, he had learned that Dunbar's real name was Fred Reis. Reis was a very tough little man, a cocky, beady-eyed

[140]

cop hater. Through O'Hare he further learned that Reis had been working in a big syndicate gambling casino just outside Miami, but that now he was supposed to be hiding out in St. Louis.

Frank managed to locate a former teller of the Pinkert State Bank who gave him a vivid description of Reis. Reis had been cashier for various gambling joints in Cicero, but he had worked primarily out of a place known as the Ship. The former teller said Fred Reis was "a little fussy . . . he would request brand-new bills." He emphasized that Fred Reis was a tough character, but he recalled that he had a slight peculiarity. He had once turned pale with terror when a cockroach showed up on a bundle of hundred-dollar bills. "He got so excited," the teller remembered, "that I didn't get the usual five-dollar tip from him that day."

That night Frank and agent Nels Tessem left Chicago and drove straight through to St. Louis to try to intercept Fred Reis, alias J. C. Dunbar, before he slipped completely from sight.

The post office inspectors in St. Louis proved helpful in letting Frank in on the fact that a special-delivery letter from Al Capone's lieutenant, Louis Lipschultz, was to be taken to Reis the following morning. Frank and Tessem tailed the mailman and followed him right in through the front door. "When Reis saw Tessem and me," Frank recalled, "he tried to slam the door, but I had my foot in the way. I handed him a subpoena to appear at the Federal Building, but he refused to accept it and threw it on the floor." Frank and Tessem arrested Reis on the spot.

As they drove over the Mississippi River bridge toward East St. Louis, Reis suddenly exploded in anger. His rage grew uncontrollable as he realized that the special-delivery letter had been sent from Capone's headquarters.

"Who are you? Show me your badges!" Reis snarled.

Frank ordered him to sit still and be quiet.

When they arrived at the Federal Building, Reis grew even more defiant. He denied ever having seen the cashier's checks or the Pinkert State Bank. Reis was unflinching, but Frank had decided on a unique way to break him.

Frank had Reis booked as a material witness and committed to a cell in a jail in Danville, Illinois. But beforehand, Frank had had the cell specially prepared for Fred Reis.

As he was led to the cell, Reis took one look at the ceiling and walls and almost choked with terror. Cockroaches were everywhere. "This ain't fit for a dog!" he screamed as he was locked in.

Frank grinned, tossing him a pack of cigarettes through the bars. "If you don't like it, tell the jailer you're willing to play ball."

"Nuts to you, copper!" Reis hissed.

Four days later Fred Reis broke down. In a state of near paranoia, he had started talking to himself, shrieking that Capone's men had let him down. He would make them regret it if it was the last thing he ever did. He pleaded to be released from the cockroach-ridden cell. All but frothing at the mouth, Reis readily admitted that he had been the cashier of the Ship in Cicero, that the boss was Al Capone, and that the cashier's checks represented Capone's *net* profits. He blurted out to Frank that in order to avoid having a lot of currency on hand, he had been instructed by his immediate superior,

Pete Penovich, to buy cashier's checks payable to himself, which he cashed whenever currency was needed.

That evening Frank wrote to U.S. Attorney Baker in East St. Louis, Illinois, who had given him assistance in jailing Reis:

We saw Reis this afternoon and he is real pleased to be released under the conditions we specified.

That same evening Frank wrote Irey:

We have secured valuable evidence from Fred Reis relating to profits from four gambling houses at Cicero in which places he was employed as cashier. He identified cashier's checks amounting to $134,000, and in his affidavit he states that this amount represents profits from the houses in 1927 and 1928. Most of these checks we have traced to bank accounts of Jack Guzik. . . . We had this witness held under a bond for $15,000, then arranged for him to be allowed to sign his own bond for $15,000 and to be released in the custody of two government agents. The witness is well pleased with this arrangement and is very friendly. He sat in jail for four days and was glad to get out. I believe he fully realized that if he had been released, his life would be in jeopardy. I have word from a confidential source* that the gang soon learned that we had found this witness, that they intended to have a $15,000 bond furnished for him. That we beat them to it by one day, that the gang is hunting for the witness with guns, and that if they find him he will not testify.

Frank spirited Reis to Chicago and sneaked him into the grand jury chambers in the middle of the night. There, Reis gave the testimony the Internal Revenue was waiting for. It put the lush profits of the Ship and

* Eddie O'Hare.

[143]

various other casinos directly into the pockets of Al Capone. Frank immediately packed Reis off to South America, notifying Irey:

I now have two Department of Justice agents with him, but their assignment expires September 17th. U.S. Attorney Johnson is trying through Assistant Attorney General Youngquist to get their assignment extended for another ten days and expects to do so. When the Department of Justice agents are called off, we will have to call on you for help. . . . It will be at least two months and perhaps four or five months before a trial will take place.

With Reis in safekeeping, Frank quickly moved against other major members of Capone's business operation. The first of these was Reis's boss, Pete Penovich. Penovich had managed several of Capone's casinos in Cicero, including the Hawthorne Smoke Shop. Subpoenaed to appear before the grand jury, Penovich was closely questioned by U.S. Attorney George E. Q. Johnson's special assistant, Dwight Green. Avoiding any mention of involvement with Al Capone, Penovich freely discussed his dealings with Reis, Ralph Capone and Jack Guzik. In 1924, he had quit the business for a short period, then had returned in 1927.

GREEN: Who got you to come back?
PENOVICH: Ralph [Capone].
GREEN: And who else?
PENOVICH: Ralph sent for me.
GREEN: What did Ralph say to you about it?
PENOVICH: Ralph asked me if I was ready to go to work and I said yes, and he said, you be here tomorrow and you can come downstairs with me and take over the management of the Subway.
GREEN: What else did he tell you about it? Whose business was it?

[144]

The Cop Hater

PENOVICH: At that time, I couldn't tell you no more whose business it was.

GREEN: What did Ralph say to you about it—who was interested there?

PENOVICH: Ralph said to me, do you want to go to work, you come down tomorrow and take charge of the Subway, so I go down the following day and I meet him over at the Hawthorne or Greyhound, and he said, you get ten percent of the place and you draw twenty-five dollars a day salary, and he took me over into the place and introduced me to Reis—Reis was cashier and had been in charge. Afterwards I got there and that is all I knew when I walked into the place in 1927.

GREEN: What did you find out later?

PENOVICH: Later Guzik took an active interest in the operating; he would call me and ask me how things were going, and I continued there during March, April, May and June, 1927.

GREEN: Now, did Guzik have anything to do with the Hawthorne Smoke Shop?

PENOVICH: Not actively.

GREEN: What do you mean by actively?

PENOVICH: We never saw him—he never gave any orders; he never spoke to anybody.

Assistant United States Attorney Samuel Clawson then took over questioning Penovich about his managership of the Hawthorne Smoke Shop, especially relative to the ledger Frank had discovered, with the notation across the top of one page, "Frank* paid $17,500 for Al." Penovich, obviously primed by the mob, insisted it represented credit to Capone for a horse bet.

CLAWSON: Well, now, this $17,500, was that the full amount of the bet that Al Capone made at that time?

PENOVICH: All I can remember at that time was what it says. He must have owed that much money in the business

* Frankie Pope.

[145]

and Frankie paid it for him. Frankie said make notation I paid so much money for Al.

CLAWSON: And if he paid that back into the business, the business had already paid it out?

PENOVICH: No, that was paid back in so this money could be distributed. If he didn't pay this $17,500, or whatever it is here, we wouldn't have enough money to pay out this amount here.

CLAWSON: Why not?

PENOVICH: Well, because if he owed this money and it was carried as cash, we would be $17,500 short, so Frankie would pay up.

CLAWSON: If Al owed it?

PENOVICH: Yes, and if Frankie would pay it, that would clean it up.

CLAWSON: Prior to Frankie's paying it, Al owed it to the business?

PENOVICH: Yes, sir. It may have been a horse transaction.

CLAWSON: Well, that is a very heavy credit, isn't it—that is a large amount of money to let anybody owe?

PENOVICH: Yes, for an ordinary person.

CLAWSON: Do you know any other person who has ever carried that heavy credit with that system?

PENOVICH: Jack Guzik.

CLAWSON: And you knew him to be one of the owners there, didn't you?

PENOVICH: No.

CLAWSON: Isn't that "J" there for Jack Guzik?

PENOVICH: The "J" and "A" is there, but I didn't know him to be one of the owners. The man had never as much as said hello to me at that time.

CLAWSON: Well, now, who authorized the credit of that amount to be extended?

PENOVICH: These credits started in a small way, and the chances are I said, how far do you want them to go? Frankie Pope knew those fellows before this, and he said, let him go as far as he wants. If I introduced somebody for credit, I would tell him what limit to put on them, and Frankie would tell me people he would introduce.

CLAWSON: How did it happen when you were just in

partnership with Frankie Pope and Dave Bates, you were taking orders from Frankie Pope?

PENOVICH: Because we had made other arrangements after we originally started. It didn't work out as I originally anticipated. I had different ideas after we started; then the change came when my fees was cut and I was told that Frankie Pope would be there with me and to cooperate with Frankie Pope and I was to run the room; he would take care of the wire.

CLAWSON: Were you given instructions that Pope was over you and would give you orders?

PENOVICH: Yes, sir. That was known as Frankie Pope's place. Ralph told me that after we had organized.

CLAWSON: And so this credit was authorized by Frankie Pope?

PENOVICH: Absolutely.

CLAWSON: Well, you know that such credit as that would only be extended to an owner of the business?

PENOVICH: No, there is other people would be that amount of money. I know people whose credit run that high.

CLAWSON: Who?

PENOVICH: I have had three or four customers who had credit that high.

CLAWSON: Well, who?

PENOVICH: Any number of bookmakers.

CLAWSON: Now that would be in the nature of a marker against Al Capone—would it be there again in distribution that would be coming to him?

PENOVICH: As we have no daily sheets—if I had the daily sheets, the previous daily sheets, I can tell whether that was a loss on the horses or whether it was money that had been borrowed that had been given to Frankie and loaned and paid back; but the way it stands now, I can't tell what the transaction was. The chances are Pope might remember it, but I couldn't tell what it was.

As Dwight Green and Samuel Clawson, the two young prosecutors from U.S. Attorney Johnson's staff, hammered away at Penovich, Frank wrote to Irey:

[147]

We have had Pete Penovich before the Grand Jury three days and will have him again Thursday. So far we have not been able to get him to satisfactorily explain the records we have, as he is attempting to make us believe that he merely made the entries at the direction of Ralph Capone and that he did not know who the interested persons were, outside of Ralph Capone, Frank Pope and Dave Bates.

He is attempting to unload everything on Ralph Capone. However, we have hopes of getting the truth out of him eventually and have some more new ammunition to use on him next week. Through information secured through phone messages in and out of the apartment where he lives with his sweetheart, Marie Moran, we know that he is reporting regularly to Al Capone after he testifies before the Grand Jury. We also have established through the phone messages that the woman Pete lives with receives many calls from men over the phone. The men set a time they will be at her apartment. She then telephones to a prostitute to come to her apartment at the appointed time. She has a good list of young girls, and she just phones to them saying, "This is Marie Moran, come over here at once." The evidence we have re this business will be used for a good purpose.

At the close of the memo, he noted:

Today I received some confidential information that Jack Guzik* feels he is carrying too much of the load of the Capone organization with his five-year jail sentence; that he doesn't like to carry all of Al's load, and that he may get to a point where he will talk about Al to help himself.

Armed with Reis's testimony, the ledger and its identification by Leslie Shumway, in addition to the statement of income submitted by Capone's attorney, Lawrence Mattingly, United States Attorney George E. Q. Johnson moved swiftly for an indictment. The grand

---

* Already imprisoned.

[148]

jury, meeting in secret session, reached a decision on March 13, 1931. For attempting to evade and defeat an income tax of $32,488.81 imposed by the Revenue Act of 1924 on a net income of $123,102.89, they indicted Al Capone for tax offenses committed in the year 1924. The indictment took effect two days prior to the expiration of the six-year statute of limitations for tax offenses committed in the year 1924. U.S. Attorney Johnson requested that the grand jury not make public its verdict until the investigation for the years 1925–1929 had been completed.

The federal grand jury convened again on June 5, this time openly. To its earlier indictment against Capone, it added another twenty-two counts covering the years 1925–1929, based on the Internal Revenue's computation of a fraction of his income for those years—totaling $1,038,655.84. Capone's tax assessment came to $219,260.12. Penalties amounted to $164,445.09.

In his memorandum summarizing the indictment, Frank wrote:

The defendant received income in the form of cash, sometimes checks, and, on many occasions, wire transfers of money by Western Union. The defendant, Alphonse Capone, had never filed a return for the years covered by the indictment and had never paid any tax on any of the income earned during those years.

The foregoing facts were established by evidence largely circumstantial in character. The defendant had no bank accounts, kept no records of activities, bought no property in his own name, and, with the exception of wire transfers of money by Western Union and an occasional check, conducted all his financial dealings with currency only. The evidence of the government, therefore, comes principally from the mouths of those who dealt either with the organization or with the defendant, and the entire situation is made clear only by piecing together many separate facts and circumstances, among which are included some admissions of income made by the defendant himself.

If found guilty on every count, Capone faced a maximum prison sentence of thirty-four years. At this point the negotiations between Capone's attorneys and U.S. Attorney Johnson became more serious. Capone's attorneys offered Attorney Johnson a compromise: their client would plead guilty to tax evasion if assured a lighter sentence. Meanwhile, the government feared that gang terrorism might yet prevent their star witnesses from testifying. In addition, there was no certainty that the Supreme Court would uphold the six-year statute of limitations. If only a three-year was held to apply, as had been the case in a recent District Court of Appeals ruling, their prosecution against Capone would be barred for all the years covered in the indictments.

Frank, concerned about the outcome if Capone should plead guilty, wrote:

Dear Mr. Irey,

The negotiations for the plea of guilty are going along slowly. The attorney representing the taxpayer indicates that the best proposition obtainable is two years. Mr. Johnson has been anxious to get at least 2-1/2 years, but I believe he is now inclined to take the two-year plea in order to get the case closed and get the defendant in the penitentiary. In event that a two-year plea is agreed upon, consideration is being given to the advisability of returning the additional indictment for *one* year only.

This idea of an additional indictment for one year only was advanced by Mr. Johnson because, if the new indictment covers several years, the persons who do not understand all the circumstances relating to this case and all the reasons for the acceptance of a guilty plea of two years might say the Gov.

did not drive a hard bargain with the defendant. For instance, it might be said he was subject to a maximum of five years each on four or five counts and the Gov. showed weakness by compromising with a plea of guilty for two years. If only two years are involved (the indictment now on record for one year and an additional indictment for one year), a two-year plea would not leave the U.S. Attorney or others open to such criticism.

Assistant Attorney General Youngquist was here early this week. Mr. Johnson informed him re the negotiations. He suggested to Mr. Johnson that he try to get the defendant also to plead guilty to an old liquor conspiracy indictment secured in 1926. That indictment was secured when agents of this Unit [Roche and Converse] were co-operating with the State's Attorney in an attempt to bring Capone back to this state to face the Chicago police for questioning re the murder of Assistant State's Attorney McSwiggin. The evidence secured at that time was not enough to warrant a prosecution of the liquor conspiracy case, and it has never been tried. The indictment served its purpose, as Capone was arrested by Roche and Converse and brought to Chicago, and as soon as he made bond in the Federal Building, he was handed over to the County police and Chicago police. They talked to him and then turned him loose.

I feel that if we go to trial, the Gov. can convict Capone in his tax case for the three years during which he was interested in the gambling house of which we have the book record, and attorneys Clawson and Froelich have stated that they feel that a conviction would result. Clawson seems anxious to try the case. Of course a bird in the hand is worth two in the bush, and I think a plea of guilty is a good outcome of any case. Will keep you informed.

Regards
Frank J. Wilson

P.S. If the guilty plea to the liquor conspiracy case can be secured in addition to the plea in the tax case, the present administration [H.H.] can tell the world that he has the biggest bootlegger and most notorious gangster in the country in jail. That ought to show the country he is doing his best for law enforcement and perhaps would result in considerable support in 1932 from the citizens who do not want "Al" to run the city of Chicago, Washington, D.C. and other places. We saw Al's picture in the Washington paper this week.

FJW

On June 18, 1931, Al Capone appeared before Federal Judge James H. Wilkerson and pleaded guilty to all counts in each indictment. Judge Wilkerson adjourned until July 30.

As the month of July began and then wore on, tension mounted in Chicago. The rest of the nation watched. Assuming, as did the entire American press, that Capone would get off with a light sentence, the *New Republic* commented: " . . . the indictment can only be described as a victory for its central figure. . . . The defeat is Chicago's." The St. Paul *News* labeled it " . . . a devastating criticism of our legal machinery."

On July 25 Frank wrote to Irey:

Mr. Johnson has been real uneasy regarding the disposition of the Al Capone case, but yesterday he was feeling much easier about it. He has the assurance that letters would come from Washington (one from Department of Justice and one from Assistant Secretary Ballantine) concurring *in the 2-1/2*-year recommendation. Yesterday Mr. Johnson informed Mellenich that the court would ask if Capone is making an *un*qualified plea, and Mellenich agreed to have the defendant state in court that it is an unqualified plea. The court has been reading that the sentence is to be 2-1/2 years; this information was given to the public by friends of the defendant. I believe the court does not care to have it appear that an agreement was made. [The judge] may feel that a statement in open court that the plea is unqualified will indicate that no previous agreement had been entered into by the court. Attorney Ahern, who

[152]

also represents Capone, was not in town yesterday, so the matter of the unqualified plea has not been passed upon by him; but Mellenich was to take Ahern to Johnson's summer home Saturday (today) for a conference.

Green, Clawson and I are uncertain what is going to happen from day to day, as the conferences Mr. Johnson has with the judge and attorneys for the defendant are only reported to us in a general way, and we are not able to determine just exactly what was intended by the judge. I wonder sometimes if anyone knows exactly what is the intention of the judge. However, I am inclined to think that the sentences will be imposed by the court on the two cases (liquor and tax) on July 30th and that the judge will follow the agreement to make the sentences as per the recommendation of the U.S. Attorney.

Clawson, Green and I have been working on a brief of some of the evidence, and the attorneys are preparing a statement of the case to be made to the court. It is not the intention to use witnesses, and no witnesses are under subpoena. They will have revenue agent Hodgins state the basis for his tax confrontation and the amount of the tax. They are talking about having me give a story of the case and emphasize the difficulties encountered during our investigation. That would not be evidence, and I have never seen that course followed in court, so I am in doubt whether the judge will be interested in our difficulties. I have made several suggestions that they determine as near as possible just what the court desires or expects, but it has not yet been settled.

The attorneys are having difficulties in preparing a correct and fair statement of the case that will show the difficulties of a prosecution in such a manner that court and press and public will not get a wrong idea that a strong case was compromised and settled for a smaller sentence than was warranted under the conditions. One rough statement was finished Friday, but it was the consensus of opinion that it sounded too much like a strong case, and Mr. Johnson requested that a new statement be prepared to carry out a different idea in order to show the difficulties of the prosecution. He requested Clawson to have the new statement ready Monday, so we worked this afternoon and will also work tomorrow (Sunday).

[153]

As the statement of the U.S. Attorney to the court is not our responsibility, I am "on the sidelines," and they are deciding how to present it and what policy to follow. I am only assisting them in getting together the evidence they decide to use. A short statement to the court re this case could not help create the impression to the public that the Gov. has a strong case. Difficulties would not be apparent until the case was on trial. In spite of any difficulties, the Gov. would get a conviction if the case was tried. The attorneys are now preparing a statement which will include and call attention to some weak points in the case and difficulties they anticipate in event of a trial.

I hope you will be here Thursday for the excitement. Will advise you if anything important turns up in the meantime.

He followed up with a memo on July 28:

Dear Mr. Irey,

Enclosed is rough draft of statement re Capone tax case. Some changes may be made tomorrow, as the final o.k. has not been placed on this one. If there are some decided changes in it I will advise you. I would suggest that you have this either photostated or copied and then return it to me via air mail. In event it becomes necessary for me to return it, I will then be able to do so. I have not said anything about sending this to you. I believe that you will get an impression from the statement that it is a strong case and that on trial a conviction would result.

The situation on the case is still very much unsettled. The attorneys [Nash and Ahern] have not indicated that they will follow the suggestions for an *un*qualified plea. Mr. Johnson said today that perhaps the court may allow the pleas of guilty to be withdrawn in event they are not unqualified. He wanted to know if we could be ready to try the tax case on October 1st if necessary and I said we could. Once a plea is made, the court cannot be required to allow it to be withdrawn, and it seems to me that the judge would be criticized if he allowed Capone to withdraw his plea and remain at liberty. I think the public wants to see Capone in jail. If Capone is at large and gangster murders occur in Chicago, the forces will be apt to call them Capone gang murders, the public will get the idea that Capone was mixed up with the murder, and the judge will be blamed for the murder because Al is at large.

I don't believe anyone can predict what the judge intends to do on Thursday. After talking to the judge several times, Mr. Johnson has reported one time that things were good and the next time that they were not so good. Then he would give his impression of what he thought the judge intended to do, and his impressions changed each time. If they make an unqualified plea, the judge may give a sentence longer than 2-1/2 years.

Clawson, Green, Froelich and I have tried hard to see if any definite conclusions could be drawn from the reports we get, but we can't say that any particular course is even likely to be followed. We are all at sea, and the four of us are mighty anxious for Thursday to come so that the decision will be made. We all agree that it is far from pleasant to be working under such unsettled and unsatisfactory conditions.

If I get anything definite I will phone you.

On July 29, the eve of his return to Judge Wilkerson's court, Capone, clad in white-bordered silk pajamas, chatted companionably with reporters in his Lexington Hotel suite. Regarding his imprisonment, Capone, posing as a martyr, mused: "I've been made an issue, and I'm not complaining. But why don't they go after all these bankers who took the savings of thousands of poor people and lost them in bank failures? How about that? Isn't it lots worse to take the last few dollars some small family had saved—perhaps to live on while the head of a family is out of a job—than to sell a little beer, a little alky?"

He prophesied an end to gang warfare. "I have always been opposed to violence—to shootings. I have fought, yes, but fought for peace."

Later that evening Capone gave a farewell dinner for his buddies and himself at the New Florence Restaurant. Mike Malone, still acting out his role as the gangster-in-hiding from Philadelphia, was invited. "Sorry you're going away, Al," he said. But Capone did not seem depressed. A two-and-a-half-year sentence with reduction for good behavior seemed easy enough to bear.

On the morning of July 30, Capone entered Judge Wilkerson's courtroom dressed in a pea-green linen suit. He was exultant as he waited for sentencing.

The sentence never came.

Wilkerson, bristling with rage, announced, "The parties to a criminal case may not stipulate as to the judgment to be entered. . . . The Court may not now say to the defendant that it will enter the judgment suggested by the prosecution."

There was a moment of stunned silence. Then Attorney Ahern leaped to his feet, his face crimson with embarrassment. "We were led to believe that the recommendation would be approved by the Court. . . . Unless we had been confident that the Court would act according to the recommendation agreed upon, the plea of guilty would never have been entered."

Wilkerson's anger mounted. "The Court will listen . . . to the recommendation of the district attorney. The Court will listen to the recommendation of the Attorney General. . . . But the thing the defendant cannot think, must not think, is that, the recommendation of the Attorney General and the Secretary of the Treasury all considered, the Court is bound to enter judgment according to that recommendation. It is time for somebody to impress upon the defendant that it is utterly impossible to bargain with a Federal Court."

Amidst the commotion that followed, the judge permitted Capone to withdraw his plea of guilty and to enter a plea of not guilty. Trial was set for early October.

On September 23, two weeks before the trial was to begin, Frank received a telephone call from Eddie O'Hare. O'Hare insisted it was urgent that they get together.

Having agreed to meet him on a street corner on the far north side of Chicago, Frank was there within an hour.

"The big fellow is going to outsmart you," O'Hare blurted.

"Don't be silly." Frank smiled, trying to retain his confidence. "We won't let Capone outsmart us."

"Oh, no? Well, the fix is in already! Capone's boys have a complete list of the prospective jurors. They're fixing them one by one. They're passing out $1,000 bills. They're promising political jobs. They're giving out tickets to prize fights. They're giving donations to churches. They're using muscle, too, Frank."

Frank tried to brush it off. "Eddie, you've been reading too many detective stories. The judge and the U.S. Attorney don't even have the jury list yet. I asked about it today."

"Oh, yeah? Well, take a look at this!"

O'Hare pushed at him a list of ten names and addresses. "There you are," he said, pointing. "They're right off the jury list—names 30 to 39."

Frank felt his heart stop as he stared at the list. It seemed incredible that his three-year-long struggle to get the case before the courts should now be defeated at the final hour!

Frank hurried the list to the office of U.S. Attorney Johnson. As Johnson studied it, he completely lost his

[157]

composure. Slamming his fist on the desk hard enough to crack the wood, he roared, "So Capone's even got the Court under his thumb! My confidence in government employees is shot to hell. Some skunk probably got a few thousand dollars for selling Capone that list."

The two men immediately hustled to the chambers of Judge Wilkerson. The strong-faced, heavyset judge listened silently as they related the story. Frank handed him the list of names.

Without moving a muscle, Wilkerson gazed at the ten names. Then he began, rationing his words as if they were precious jewels: "I do not have my jury list yet. I do not believe it wise for me to ask for it, lest I engender suspicion. We will sit tight and wait for it to come to me in due course. I shall call you gentlemen when I get it."

That night Frank met again with Eddie O'Hare, who had more news to report. "Capone and his gang are not worrying about the trial, Frank. They've got the entire jury list parceled out in lots of five and ten names. Some of the biggest shots in town have their quotas to work on. When they get through, every prospective juror on the panel will be either beholden to Capone or so scared that the trial will be over before it gets started."

Frank felt too defeated to say anything.

The next morning Wilkerson sent for Frank, U.S. Attorney Johnson and Art Madden. The ten names on the list Eddie O'Hare had given Frank tallied exactly with names 30 to 39 on the panel.

But for some reason the big judge did not appear ruffled. "Bring your case into court as planned, gentlemen," he said quietly. "Leave the rest to me."

PART III

"The attention of the country will be commanded to-morrow by the trial of Al Capone as an income tax evader, which begins in Federal Judge James H. Wilkerson's court at 10 A.M. It will be the most famous of all the prosecutions of gang chieftains produced by the Volstead era and comparable in interest to the Loeb-Leopold trial. Federal prosecutors headed by United States Attorney George E. Q. Johnson completed their preparations for the trial Saturday night, ending three years of unrelenting investigation born of a zeal to rid Chicago of its foremost public enemy. Seventy-five witnesses are under subpoena to give evidence of Capone's alleged $1,038,654 booze, gambling and vice income over a six-year period, on which he paid no taxes. . . . Agents of the intelligence unit which developed the income tax case against Capone expressed themselves as certain of a conviction. Most valuable for the government probably will be Fred Reis. . . ."

—From the front page of the Chicago *Tribune*,
Monday, October 5, 1931.

13
THE TRIAL

On the eve of the Capone trial, Damon Runyon interviewed the gang lord at a table at Colosimo's Café, where he sat surrounded by a coterie of gangsters, politicians and lawyers. How did Capone estimate his chances? Runyon asked him. Capone grinned. "I believe I've got at least an even break."

The following morning Judith Wilson prepared for her husband his favorite breakfast, baked pears. He was wearing a rather loud red and green necktie which she insisted he change, pointing out that he'd better dress more conservatively when appearing in court. Frank held no illusions about what lay ahead. Besides the fact that Capone now had the jury in the palm of his hand, the *New York Times* had reported: "In government circles it was predicted the gangleader would probably receive the minimum penalty of three years"—barely a slap on the face to the man who had controlled Chicago's underworld for a decade.

Frank had hurriedly written to Elmer Irey six months before: "Of course a bird in the hand is worth

[161]

two in the bush, and I think a plea of guilty is a good outcome of any case." But now he no longer felt that way. If in two and a half years Capone was free and back running Chicago exactly as before, the overall effect would be disastrous. No court would have the power to try him again. If any should try, it would appear that Capone was a martyr, a victim of federal harassment.

To many, Capone had already become a legendary figure, a symbol of the times, as Damon Runyon had noted in a dispatch the day before: "It is impossible to talk to Capone without conceding that he has that intangible attribute known as personality, or, as we say in the world of sport, 'color.' " But to Frank, Capone would always epitomize the stranglehold of crime at its most barbaric. He had only to recall the image of Scalise, Anselmi and Giunta being beaten to death by Capone with a baseball bat; the gunning down of Jake Lingle, McSwiggin and the others who had been murdered, tortured or clubbed into submission—as well as the attempt on his own life only a few months before. As Frank ate his breakfast that morning, he felt very grim. Almost three years of his and Judith's life had perhaps been wasted. A victory for Capone would open the door to an era of crime unparalleled in the country's history. It would illustrate to every small-time criminal and thug that even the federal courts could be "controlled"—that any juror was corruptible.

Yet, he had no power over the events that were to follow. He had secured the evidence and the witnesses; now it was up to U.S. Attorney Johnson and his staff. There was no guarantee that the Court would even uphold the indictment. Tax evasion was still an extremely sophisticated charge. Even though the convictions of Nitti, Guzik and the others had been secured, none of these men were so adept at covering their trail or so powerful in the public mind as Capone himself.

It seemed ludicrous that a man who was responsible for at least five hundred deaths, whose vicious beatings and tortures were common knowledge, who had become America's number-one symbol of vice and corruption, should have been behind bars only once: In Philadelphia in May 1929 Capone had been caught carrying a pistol. He had been sentenced to a year's imprisonment.

What disturbed Frank even more, however, was that if Capone should walk out of the courtroom, acquitted, he would be, in a sense, sinless. Not only would his deeds go unpunished, but he would demonstrate that the laws of the United States were impotent, that its citizens were at the mercy of the underworld.

And of course Capone knew this.

By 9:30 A.M. a procession of squad cars carrying fourteen heavily armed detectives raced across town, conveying the massive figure of Capone the three miles from the Lexington Hotel to the seventy-year-old federal courthouse bound by Clark, Dearborn, Adams and Jackson streets in the heart of Chicago. The lead car paused at each intersection so that its occupants could survey the side streets, alert for any of Capone's henchmen who might attempt to rescue him. Approaching the Federal Building, the motorcade turned into a tunnel normally used only by delivery trucks, there to wait until Capone could be safely transported by freight elevator up to the courtroom on the sixth floor.

When Frank arrived at the courthouse at 9:45 A.M., the steps and entrances to the building reminded him of morning at the circus. Pickpockets were busy, but the police had begun arresting them. Fighting his way

[163]

through crowds of clamoring reporters, photographers and sob sisters, Frank tripped over tripods and microphone wires, the soles of his shoes crunching down hard on a carpet of flash bulbs. What was reportedly the largest group of press and radio correspondents ever to cover a criminal trial surged in through the front doors, up stairs, down hallways, finally streaming into the ancient trial chambers.

Frank followed them in and took a seat at the table with U.S. Attorney George E. Q. Johnson. Assembled at the same table were Johnson's four young assistants, Samuel Clawson, Jacob I. Grossman, Dwight H. Green and William Froelich. To the right of them, at the counsels' table, sat Capone's two attorneys, Michael J. Ahern and Albert Fink. Capone's lawyers presented a fascinating contrast—Ahern, tall and elegant, sitting next to the little, almost Dickensian Albert Fink, round-bellied and fat-faced, his gold-rimmed eyeglasses riding the tip of his pointed nose.

Within a few moments Capone sauntered into the courtroom dressed in a mustard-colored suit and yellow tie. Mountains of pasta and Niagaras of Chianti had deposited layers of fat on his five-foot ten-and-a-half-inch body, but the muscle beneath the fat was rock-hard. He moved with an aggressive forward thrust, his shoulders meaty and sloping like a bull's. Accompanying him was his trim, tight-lipped bodyguard, Phil D'Andrea. Capone beamed to the crowd as he took his seat at the counsel table only a few feet from Frank. He appeared to notice Frank out of the corner of his eye, but he gave no sign of recognition as D'Andrea fussed over him, adjusted his chair and plucked a loose thread from his beefy shoulders.

Frank's pulse missed a beat as he stared across at

Capone's bribed jurors, then back at Capone's beaming face.

Judge Wilkerson now entered the court. He wore no robe over his dark blue business suit. His deep-set eyes and oval face were expressionless. He took his seat on the extreme edge of a swivel chair. He was handsome, in his early fifties, his iron-gray hair loose and parted slightly to the right and combed over to one side. Nervously gazing above at the ceiling and walls, Frank noticed that they were covered with murals depicting scenes from the American Revolution. Behind the judge's bench Benjamin Franklin addressed the Continental Congress, his right hand outstretched toward George Washington—a chilling contrast to the sordid proceedings about to begin below. The windows were too high up and too narrow to admit sufficient light, so electric bulbs in chandeliers and sconces burned everywhere throughout the courtroom.

Frank waited, tensely eyeing the jurors. Judge Wilkerson glanced at the panel, then summoned the bailiff to the bench. In a crisp, stern voice he snapped, "Judge Edwards has another trial commencing today. Go to his courtroom and bring me his entire panel of jurors. Take my entire panel to Judge Edwards."

Frank stared at Wilkerson in amazement. Out of the corner of his eye he glimpsed Capone's face. Its features had clouded with fury, but Capone did not make a move. There was a sudden stir as scores of photographers rushed through the courtroom and began shooting pictures from all angles—on top of the bench, from the windowsills, from the jury box. Wilkerson then announced that no further courtroom pictures would be permitted.

As the morning wore on, a new jury was empaneled.

Both sides used all their peremptory challenges. Judge Wilkerson shortened the procedure by questioning the veniremen himself, although accepting suggestions for questions from both the prosecution and the defense. The new jury was made up mostly of small-towners, all middle-aged or elderly: a farmer, a lubricating engineer, a wood patenter, a country storekeeper, an insurance agent, a painter, an abstractor, a retired hardware dealer, a shop worker, a real estate agent. They all swore that they harbored no prejudice against Alphonse Capone and had no wish to see him imprisoned. Nine of the twelve had served as jurors before.

Damon Runyon described the scene:

Capone's chief counsel, Ahern, a tall good-looking chap of perhaps middle age, who wore a gray suit and tan shoes, approached the railing in front of the bench . . . flanked by his associate in the defense, Albert Fink, a ruddy-faced baldish man given to easy attitudes.

Ahern expressed his dissatisfaction with the jurors, wanting them all dismissed, stating that he preferred some who were closer to the metropolitan atmosphere. But Wilkerson quietly overruled him.

Runyon described the feeling in the courtroom:

'Twas a warmish morning, and Al, being stout, is susceptible to the heat. His soft collar was already crumpled. He frequently mopped his forehead with a white handkerchief. His swarthy jowls had been newly shaved. His black hair, now getting quite sparse, was plastered back on his skull. . . . Judge Wilkerson himself is a fine-looking man with iron-gray hair. His eyebrows are black and strong. He wore no flowing robe, like New York judges. He was dressed in a quiet business suit. . . . Wilkerson made it clear to the men in the jury box that Capone is being tried on charges of violating the income tax law and nothing else.

Other members of the press noted that Wilkerson referred to the defendant politely as "Mr. Capone."

When the first day's proceedings ended at 4:00 P.M., Frank was certain that none of the new jurors had as yet been intimidated.

Arriving in court the following morning, he watched assistant prosecutor Dwight Green rise to submit the government's case. But before Green could begin, the court was suddenly disrupted by Defense Attorney Fink, who announced that he had learned that one of the twelve men sworn in as jurors should be disqualified for "serious reasons." Fink would not publicly say why he felt the man unfit, but Wilkerson excused the jury and ordered Fink to meet with U.S. Attorney Johnson and his staff and report to him what they decided.

After a brief discussion, Wilkerson conferred with the attorneys, and the jury remained intact. No explanation was made. Green began again.

Green recounted the charges against the defendant, whom he referred to as Alphonse Capone, alias Al Capone, alias Scarface Al, alias Scarface Capone, alias Al Brown, alias Scarface Brown, alias A. Costa. Then he listed the twenty-three counts against Capone and the varying sums of alleged income and tax liability for the years 1924 to 1929. Green asserted that the evidence would show that "certain gambling interests in Cicero, with which the defendant was connected" realized net profits of $320,000 in 1924, $117,000 in 1925, $170,000 in 1926, and huge sums in 1927, 1928 and 1929.

Green stated that late in 1927 Capone had rented a "palatial home in Florida" and paid $20,000 for a six-months' season. He added that Capone later paid $40,000 for a large estate in Florida and expended more than $100,000 for its maintenance and improvements.

U.S. Attorney Johnson then called the government's first witness, Charles W. Arndt, an Internal Revenue collector who testified to the total absence of any income tax returns in his office from Alphonse Capone from 1924 to 1929.

Chester Bragg followed, identifying himself as an insurance salesman from Berwyn, Illinois. He was asked by Dwight Green to point out the defendant, and he aimed a finger at Capone. Bragg was later described by the press as "a neat, deep-chested, determined-looking citizen."

Bragg recalled the vigilante raid on the Hawthorne Smoke Shop. He then testified that after the gambling machines had been confiscated and loaded in trucks, he was attacked by a crowd of men. He had been assigned to guard the front door, he said, and Capone "came on the run from somewhere nearby* and began pushing on the door to get in."

"I asked him, 'What do you think this is, a party?' and he replied, 'I'm the owner of this place.'"

Defense Attorney Ahern cross-examined Bragg, apparently testing his memory. Bragg repeated that at the time of the raid on the Hawthorne Smoke Shop, Capone had been there and had said that he was the owner of the place. Bragg also restated that his nose was broken by a blow from a blackjack or brass knuckles.

Ahern asked: "How many persons beat you?"

"About a thousand tried, but I don't know how many did," Bragg answered.

---

* From the Hawthorne Inn across the street.

[168]

The Trial

David Morgan, described by the press as "a man of ruddy complexion with a pince-nez," followed Bragg to the stand. After he had given his testimony concerning the raid on the Hawthorne Smoke Shop, Attorney Fink cross-examined him as to his knowledge of the difference in size between Al Capone and his brother Ralph, obviously trying to establish a case of mistaken identity.

FINK: Did this man who admitted ownership of the place have any marks on his face?
MORGAN: Yes, he had some scars.
FINK: Which side?

Morgan took a swift peek at Al Capone. Fink snapped: "Don't look at him."

"The left side," replied Morgan quickly.

Al Capone grinned.

The next witness was the Reverend Henry Hoover, who had led the raid on the Hawthorne Smoke Shop following William McSwiggin's murder. At the request of Attorney Green he pointed out Al Capone and testified to the statements made by Capone at the time of the raid. Capone had entered the gaming room and demanded of Hoover: "What are you always picking on me for? Can't I run a place in Cicero? You've pulled the last raid that you're going to pull on me!" He then implored: "If you will let up on me in Cicero, I will withdraw from Stickney." * But Reverend Hoover stated that he had refused to bargain with Capone. He told him: "You must obey the law or get out of the western suburbs."

Reverend Hoover was asked by Attorney Fink if the citizens' organization that did the raiding was still in existence.

* The adjoining suburb.

[169]

"No," he replied.

Finally it was time for Leslie Adelbert Shumway.

Pale and shaky, the polelike Shumway perched himself on the edge of the witness chair only a few feet from Capone and his bodyguard D'Andrea, who stared at him menacingly, as if they were about to murder him at any moment.

Assistant U.S. Attorney Grossman began the interrogation. Shumway admitted he had been the cashier at the Hawthorne Smoke Shop for a period of two years.

GROSSMAN: Who were the managers of the place?

SHUMWAY: Mr. Penovich and Mr. Pope.

GROSSMAN: Mr. Pope?

SHUMWAY: Frankie Pope.

GROSSMAN: And just what kind of a place was that gambling establishment—what did they have there?

SHUMWAY: Well, they had the horses and all kinds of gambling games, a wheel, craps, twenty-one, birdcage.

GROSSMAN: Well, was it a pretty complete gambling establishment?

SHUMWAY: Why, yes, sir, I should say so.

GROSSMAN: What were your duties at that place?

SHUMWAY: I was figuring sheets.

GROSSMAN: Sheets on what?

SHUMWAY: The horses.

FINK: You were what?

GROSSMAN: He figured the sheets on the horses.

SHUMWAY: Figured the sheets on the bets.

GROSSMAN: Well, did you do anything other than figure sheets before you became cashier?

SHUMWAY: Yes, sir, I used to help Mr. Penovich figure up.

GROSSMAN: Figure?

SHUMWAY: Figure up the day's business.

GROSSMAN: Now, just tell us what that consisted of.

SHUMWAY: Well, that was held on one sheet.

The Trial

Prosecutor Grossman led Shumway into a detailed description of the daily sheets. The sheets, Shumway testified, were destroyed every two or three months, when they had filled the steel chest in which they were kept. At this point the ledger Frank had discovered in the old filing cabinet in the Post Office Building was introduced. It was identified as a thirty-four-page loose-leaf book that contained a series of daily reports which had not been destroyed. Shumway then identified the handwriting in the ledger as his own.

GROSSMAN: I notice a figure at the top left-hand corner of each page—for instance on page 12—"bank $12,000." What does that mean?

SHUMWAY: That was the bankroll that we started with.

GROSSMAN: Started at the beginning of the month?

SHUMWAY: Yes.

GROSSMAN: In other words, that was the capital of the business?

SHUMWAY: Yes, sir.

Shumway then went on to estimate the Hawthorne Smoke Shop profits for the two years he was cashier. They exceeded $550,000.

GROSSMAN: Now, you stated a little while ago that Mr. Penovich and Mr. Pope were the managers?

SHUMWAY: Yes, sir.

GROSSMAN: They were sort of bosses right over you?

SHUMWAY: Yes, sir.

GROSSMAN: Who was the boss over them?

FINK (interrupting): If there was one.

GROSSMAN: If there was one.

FINK: And if he knows. That is really a conclusion, if Your Honor please.

[171]

WILKERSON: It may or it may not be. It may be a fact, if he knows.

FINK: My point is this: There may have been some things done and said from which he would draw some one conclusion and Your Honor might draw another.

WILKERSON: You have the right to cross-examine him on that. I say that is a fact as the question is put.

There followed an effort by the government to prove that Shumway had actually been told that Capone owned the place. Shumway grew ill at ease. He twisted his neck and cleared his throat. At times his voice became very weak. He could not testify that he had personal knowledge as to the ownership of the place. Grossman kept maneuvering throughout most of the afternoon, trying to get a positive answer from Shumway as to the ownership, but Shumway could only fall back on hearsay, to which Defense Attorney Fink objected immediately.

Finally Judge Wilkerson leaned across the desk and asked Shumway: "Do you know who the owner of the place was?"

"Not definitely," Shumway replied, nervously eyeing Capone.

Wilkerson persisted: "Did you know from the conduct of anyone around there whose place it might be? Did you see anyone conducting himself as if he might be the proprietor giving orders?"

Shumway shook his head.

He had seen Al Capone in the place, and Capone sometimes bet on the horses over the wire. He had seen his name on the books recording such transactions. At day's end, Shumway carried the money from the establishment to the bank, and once he had a conversation with Capone: "Capone asked me what I would do if I

The Trial

were held up while taking money to the safe. I told him I'd let them have the money, and he said, 'That's right.' "

The cross-examination was brief. Ahern asked Shumway if he was getting any money from the government or if he had been promised any. Shumway answered no.

When the session ended at 4:15 P.M., Capone waited in the courtroom for the photographers in the hallway outside to set up their equipment in order to photograph him. Within an hour newspapers across the nation carried the headline: "U.S. Fails To Trace Gambling Profits To Capone."

The following morning, October 8, Assistant U.S. Attorney Clawson introduced Lawrence Mattingly's letter admitting Capone's taxable income. Mattingly's actions were instantly attacked by attorneys Fink and Ahern. "A lawyer cannot confess for his client," Fink objected heatedly. "When my client conferred power of attorney in this case to enable him to keep out of the penitentiary, it did not imply the power of authority to make statements that may get him into the penitentiary."

"It might have that effect ultimately," retorted Wilkerson.

Then came the moment Frank had been awaiting. Assistant U.S. Attorney Clawson called him to the stand. It was noted by the *Tribune* that "Wilson was the first witness at the trial to speak in tones audible as far as the press table."

Frank testified that Mattingly had told him on April 10, 1930, that Capone paid no tax but was willing to pay.

"I told him," Frank explained, "that our office could give no immunity, but I offered to listen to anything he had to say. Mr. Mattingly then arranged to bring Capone in. On April 17, Mr. Mattingly came into the office, and a

[173]

little later Capone entered with two men I did not know."

Then Prosecutor Clawson, over defense objections, read to the jury the stenographic transcript of the interview. When this was completed, Clawson directed Frank's attention to one of Capone's answers in the interview in which he evaded a question by referring the question to his lawyer.

CLAWSON: When he said this, what gesture did he make?
WILSON: He waved at Mr. Mattingly.
CLAWSON: Now, did you see Mr. Mattingly after that?
WILSON: I did. On September 19, 1930.
CLAWSON: Who was present?
WILSON: Revenue Agent Hodgins, Mr. Mattingly and myself. Mr. Mattingly said that he had consulted with Mr. Capone and his associates and had got some data and figures together and would bring them in.

The next day, Frank continued, Mattingly returned, and they retired to Wilson's private office.

WILSON: Mr. Mattingly said it was difficult to get the facts and figures together. He took some papers from his inside coat pocket, and while turning them over, he would look out of the window and talk very slowly and deliberately. Finally he threw the papers over to me. He said, "This is the best we can do. Mr. Capone is willing to pay the tax on these figures."
CLAWSON: Are these the papers? [offering Wilson the evidence]
WILSON: They are.

Over more objections from Fink and Ahern, Clawson offered Mattingly's statement in evidence. Instantly Fink began shouting. "This is the last toe! They have got him nailed to the cross now! This is just putting the last toe on him now! I do not want to waive it, but I think that

[174]

in justice to the defendant Your Honor ought to overrule the objection to this matter and let the whole thing go in now, because there are some things in this letter that at least indicate the lawyer is crazy!"

With that, Attorney Ahern interjected: "The Supreme Court has often held that it is human nature to avoid tax. We had a Boston tea party—"

"I suppose," chided Wilkerson, "this is a Boston tea party."

Wilkerson proceeded to excuse the jury. He then adjusted his glasses and carefully examined Mattingly's letter. Finally he looked up. "There are a lot of things that raise a question in my mind about the admission of that letter. It is perfectly clear—the law—with regard to that letter. Did Mattingly, under the scope of authority, have authority to say all the things that are in that letter? He had authority to settle and adjust taxes. Had he authority to do anything more? And there is so much extraneous matter in that letter that you cannot separate it as far as the taxes."

Clawson and Ahern then began a side discussion with the revenue agents as to the data of the Capone interview. The discussion suddenly erupted into an argument. In the midst of this, Judge Wilkerson announced that he did not consider it necessary to rule on the admissibility of the letter at that moment. Rather, he said, he would allow the prosecution to offer the letter, and he would rule on it the following morning.

Clawson then offered to present the letter in evidence, with everything deleted except statements bearing on Capone's income and its sources. Again Ahern objected to the admission of the letter.

By this time the two attorneys had risen from their seats and were beginning to threaten each other physically. At this point Judge Wilkerson interrupted the altercation and ordered Clawson and Ahern to their seats. He then proceeded to present his ruling:

There is a difference between the admissibility of this document in a suit—say the United States were suing the defendant for a definite amount of tax—there is a difference between the admissibility of the document in that kind of a suit and its admissibility in a suit of this kind, for the purpose of showing that the statement was made, not for the purpose of establishing the fact set forth in that statement; but the fact that this attorney brought in his statement after this interview in the office of the collector is a relevant fact in this case. And without reference to its being proof of the things that are therein stated, he went out with the knowledge of the defendant, with the understanding that he was to bring something back. Whether this is proof of the things or thing there stated is one question; whether it is admissible as an act or thing is an entirely different question in a criminal case.

"In other words, Your Honor," attorney Fink broke in, "you admit the letter and instruct the jury that the contents of the letter are no proof of the things—"

"Of the things there stated," Wilkerson replied. "But as far as being an act in this case, an act by the agent of the defendant, something done with his knowledge, that is something to be considered in this case. My view is that it is admissible on that theory and that its effect is something to be controlled by the character of the court's instructions to the jury after all the evidence is in. That will be the ruling of the court. The objection is overruled."

The jury was then brought back into the courtroom. The *Tribune* reported, "The defense did not choose to cross-examine Agent Wilson."

The Trial

That evening Capone had two new suits tailored for him in his suite at the Hotel Lexington. "You don't need to be ordering fancy duds," remarked fellow gangster Frankie Rio. "Why don't you have a suit made with stripes on it? You're going to prison."

"The hell I am!" Capone retorted. "I'm going to Florida for a nice, long rest, and I need some new clothes before I go."

Capone's hopes ran high. He was certain that his two attorneys, who charged such high fees, who had saved him time and again, would, in the end, get him off.

On Friday, October 9, the Chicago *Herald-Examiner* reported that the cost of wholesale alcohol had jumped from $30 to $32 per five-gallon can. It ascribed the rise to the cost of Al Capone's defense.

The following morning Capone arrived in court wearing a new green hat, a grayish overcoat with brown velvet collar, a dark gray suit, bright yellow shoes, and a diamond-flecked watch chain which extended across the front of his portly vest. His bodyguard, Phil D'Andrea, sat down quietly next to him, fixing his eyes on the witness stand.

The first witness, Parker Henderson, was sworn in. Henderson was noticeably uneasy as he glanced at D'Andrea, but he proceeded to narrate in detail the purchase of the Palm Island estate, which had been made in his name. Later, he stated, he transferred the property to Mrs. Mae Capone, Al's wife.

He then admitted signing numerous Western Union money transfers and turning the money over to Capone. These were generally for sums of $1,000 to $5,000. After Capone moved to Palm Island, he testified, the money came in batches anywhere from $600 to $5,000. Some of

[177]

the Western Union transfers were to Albert Capone, a brother, but Henderson related that Alphonse Capone endorsed most of them.

For the first time, actual money was traced to the pockets of Capone. Henderson went on to identify the Western Union money orders themselves (submitted by the prosecution as evidence), totaling more than $30,000, which he said he cashed for Capone. In addition, he estimated that another $80,000 in money orders had been made out to and cashed by "Albert Costa"—a Capone alias.

The next witness, John Fotre, manager of the Western Union office in the Lexington Hotel, testified that he did not know who had sent the money orders. His testimony was startling to Frank. In a pretrial conference, Fotre had named the sender and had promised to disclose that information to the Court. Judge Wilkerson warned him grimly, "You better think this over."

When court recessed, Frank grabbed Fotre in the hallway and pulled him into the judge's chambers. Fotre turned chalk-white as Frank interrogated him. "What can you expect," Fotre finally said defensively, "when one of Capone's hoodlums sits there with his hand on his gun?"

The following morning Frank met with Judge Wilkerson and apprised him of D'Andrea's tactic. Wilkerson's first concern was to avoid terrorizing those witnesses who had yet to testify. He instructed Frank to handle D'Andrea outside the courtroom. He would adjourn the trial for a few moments during the morning session to give Frank an opportunity to lure D'Andrea into the corridor.

At a prearranged signal, the bailiff whispered to

D'Andrea that a messenger was waiting in the corridor with a message for him. As D'Andrea left the courtroom, Frank followed him out. D'Andrea headed down the hallway. As he passed Judge Wilkerson's chamber, Frank, joined by two fellow agents, charged him, shoving him inside the judge's chambers.

"Give me that gun!" Frank roared.

D'Andrea stiffened, then stuttered something, slipping a .38 caliber revolver from his hip pocket.

"Give me those bullets!"

D'Andrea quickly handed him the cartridges, then flourished his deputy sheriff's credentials, which had been supplied by Mayor Big Bill Thompson's office.

"You're under arrest!" Frank spun D'Andrea around and pushed him back down the corridor into the courtroom.

"Your Honor," Attorney Ahern pleaded, trying to appease Wilkerson as D'Andrea was led before him, "this defendant has taken care of his mother and sisters. . . . If Your Honor understood D'Andrea's mind and his heart, you would know that he did not mean any affront to the court." Attorney Fink pointed out that as a deputy sheriff D'Andrea had a right to carry a pistol and had "probably carried it into Federal Court unthinkingly."

But the judge was not to be taken in. Addressing D'Andrea before the assembled jury and spectators, he began:

The court would have been blind indeed if it had not observed the intimidation practiced on the witnesses almost under the eyes of the court. It must be borne in mind that this respondent was sitting with his concealed firearms behind the defendant [Capone], while the defendant was glaring at witnesses who were on the point of remembering something about the business in which the defendant was engaged, and which the witnesses could not possibly have forgotten.

Wilkerson then cited D'Andrea for contempt of court.

During the luncheon recess, Capone growled to reporters, "I don't care what happens to D'Andrea. He's a damn fool. I don't care if he gets a month or ten years."

Wilkerson sentenced D'Andrea to six months in federal prison. The trial again got under way.

Witnesses now appeared who had sold things to Capone: real estate agents, decorators, tailors, jewelers, butchers, bakers, furniture dealers, building contractors . . .

In the corridor a strikingly pretty brunette secretary from the Miami Western Union office, imported by the government to testify, icily expressed her disenchantment with Chicago. "What do y'all do for excitement up here?" she drawled.

The parade of witnesses continued. They told about Capone's $200-a-week meat purchases, his $39,000 telephone bill over a four-year period, his purchase of a custom-made shirt with an extra-strong pistol pocket for $135, improvements on his Miami estate totaling $50,000, and $12,000 spent on a gold-plated dinner service. A Mr. James Banken of Marshall Field's testified that Capone bought shirts costing from $22 to $30 apiece, with the monograms $1 each. His ties cost $4 each and his handkerchiefs $2.75; according to Mr. Banken, Capone bought them by the bunch. Capone even wore silk union suits at $12 each.

Fink interrogated Banken, who had described the union suits as fine silk "like a lady's glove."

FINK: Were they warm?
BANKEN: No, not warm. Just a nice suit of underwear.
FINK: How much are they now?
BANKEN: Ten dollars.

"Aha!" snorted Fink. "They've gone down?"

"Yes," Banken replied, "two dollars." A columnist quipped, "It looked for a moment as if he had a sale."

Oscar De Feo of Marshall Field's remembered making more than twenty suits for Capone, plus a dozen topcoats, along with suits for four or five of Capone's friends, altogether totaling $3,600.

Samuel J. Steinberg, a jeweler, told of the batch of thirty diamond belt buckles Capone purchased at $273 apiece, or $8,190 for the lot.* One of the gleaming diamond belt buckles was then flashed before the jury. Each buckle, according to Steinberg, was engraved with the initials of the recipient.

Fink promptly questioned the quality of the belt buckles, trying to raise the point that Capone might have been gypped. But he was quickly stopped by Wilkerson, who interjected: "The goods make no difference. It is immaterial whether the defendant got value received or not as long as he spent the money."

Steinberg then recalled the day that Capone stopped in Marshall Field's and bought twenty-two beaded bags at $22.50 apiece.

Capone often grinned at the testimony, especially when they discussed his underwear. And when Attorney Grossman passed around the belt buckle, Capone examined it with as much apparent interest as if he had never seen it before.

* Jake Lingle was wearing one of these buckles when he was shot to death.

A parade of furniture dealers followed, admitting they had furnished Capone's Palm Island home and his Prairie Avenue house, where Capone's mother lived, with chairs, sofas, tables, beds and rugs worth $26,000.

Fred Avery, former manager of the Metropole Hotel, testified that he had asked Capone to pay for the eight rooms he occupied there. "The next day he paid the bill—I think it was about $3,000. He paid it in cash from his pants pocket.

"He had a banquet the night of the Dempsey-Tunney fight," Avery went on. "It lasted two nights. The bill for $3,000 included food and some incidentals. Capone furnished his own entertainment."

Morrisey Smith, clerk and cashier of the Metropole Hotel, stated that Capone had occupied his eight-room suite there from 1925 to 1928.* Attorney Grossman interrogated Mr. Smith:

"Who paid for this suite of eight rooms?"

"Mr. Capone," Smith replied.

Smith then related that Capone always paid in cash, sometimes with bills as high as $500. Three or four other men usually occupied the suite with Capone. In addition, there were usually at least half a dozen other rooms where guests of Capone stayed.

Fink objected to this testimony. "I thought the government had to prove his income, not his outgo."

Wilkerson said with a smile, "It would appear what you pay out is at least a circumstance to show that you get something in."

A Mr. H. J. Etheritz testified that Capone had purchased "$800 worth of linen and kitchen utensils for his

---

* Capone had registered at the Metropole as "Mr. Al Ross."

estate" from the Miami department store with which Etheritz was affiliated.

The landscaping job on the Florida estate had been done by Joseph A. Brower, who said he had received $2,100 for it. "Part of the payment was made in checks signed by Jake Guzik. Mr. Capone told me Guzik was his financial secretary."

H. F. Ryder, who had built the dock and boathouse for Capone's Palm Island estate, recalled:

"I saw money wrappers marked $1,000 lying around the house. A couple of handfuls, I guess. There was enough money in a cupboard to choke an ox. Mrs. Capone got $250 out of there to pay me a bill. She paid me in fifty-dollar bills, and the roll was about as big as your wrist."

Henry E. Keller, a dock foreman for Capone at his Palm Island estate, admitted that Capone paid him a salary of $550 a month. He recalled that on one occasion when he and Capone had lunch together, Capone had asked him where he was born. "In the old Tenth Ward," Keller had replied.

"Is that so?" Capone remarked. "Why, I came from New York. I got my start as a bartender in Coney Island."

Vernon Hawthorne, who was state's attorney of the Eleventh Florida District in 1928, related an interview between Capone and Miami officials in the summer of that year. The authorities, he said, had objected to Capone's presence there and wanted to know "what he proposed to do in Miami."

"I'm just here for a rest," he quoted Capone as saying.

Capone had at first refused to say what his business was, Hawthorne testified, but later he said he was in the cleaning and pressing business, real estate and gambling.

The witness said he finally asked Capone whether gambling was not his principal business. He quoted Capone as remarking, "Well, yes."

The trial session ended at 3:40 P.M. When Capone left, hands thrust in pockets, smiling jauntily, he was described by the press as "unworried."

Later, he attended the Northwestern–Notre Dame football game at Soldier Field, accompanied by his bodyguards and a city official, Alderman A. J. Prignano. That evening, Italian historical novelist Rafael Sabatini, about to embark on an American lecture tour, was asked in an interview his opinion of Capone. He reflected that Capone was "a center of that atmosphere of treachery, intrigue, shots in the dark and raw power in which historical romance best grows," but he disqualified him as a proper subject for the genre because "he seems really to have no ideals." Instead, he predicted that Mussolini would probably emerge as the most inspiring personality of the day, for "the power and the intrigue are there, and the ideal with them."

On October 14, the prosecution called its last key witness, Fred Reis. Frank was certain that Reis would cooperate; he had no other choice if he wanted the government's protection. Reis was questioned by Assistant U.S. Attorney Jacob I. Grossman. He did not fidget or shudder, as Shumway had done, nor did Capone try to stare him down. Instead, according to the Chicago *Tribune*'s account, "Capone sat erect and listened with interest."

GROSSMAN: Were you the cashier of the Subway, a gambling house at 4738 West 22nd Street, Cicero, in 1927?
REIS: Yes.
GROSSMAN : Who managed it?

[184]

REIS: Pete Penovich.

GROSSMAN: Did you ever see the defendant Alphonse Capone there?

REIS: No.

GROSSMAN: Did you operate anywhere else during that year?

REIS: Yes, we operated the Ship, early in the year and again in September.

GROSSMAN: Did you see the defendant there?

REIS: Yes, sir.

GROSSMAN: What was he doing?

REIS: He was in the telegraph operator's office talking to Jack Guzik.

GROSSMAN: Did you see him in the place you operated known as the Radio?

REIS: Yes. I was taking bets at the counter. He came by and said, "Hello, Reis." I said, "Hello, Al."

GROSSMAN: What did you do with the profits of the place you operated?

REIS: I purchased cashier's checks with them and turned them over to Bobby Barton [Guzik's chauffeur]. He took them to Jack Guzik.

GROSSMAN: What were the total profits during 1927?

REIS: I don't remember exactly—around $150,000.

The *Tribune* noted that Reis neither stared at the defendant nor avoided his eyes, but watched the prosecutor, answering each question firmly.

GROSSMAN: I show you cashier's checks purchased from the Pinkert State Bank, Cicero. Tell us about those checks.

REIS: I bought them with cash representing profits from the house and turned them over to Bobby Barton.

Grossman read to the jurors the names on the checks. They had been made payable to "J. C. Dunbar." Reis admitted that Dunbar was his alias.

[185]

Grossman offered the checks in evidence, but Fink objected.

"They relate to enterprises with which the defendant must have had some connection," countered Judge Wilkerson, carefully examining one of the checks. "His name appears on this one."

The courtroom suddenly fell silent. It was the first disclosure that Capone had endorsed one of the checks. Capone, who had boasted of never signing anything, glanced up sharply.

Attorney Fink, caught off guard, examined the check. Finally, he stated for the record, "The check is endorsed by J. C. Dunbar, and underneath is the signature of Al Capone."

That morning the *New York Times* had reported:

A fund of $100,000 is being collected to defend Scarface Alphonse Capone, Chicago gangleader, in the Federal Courts, it was learned today. Bookmakers in this city and in the suburbs of Chicago are being levied upon by the simple expedients of highway robbery, friendly "rides," and assessments against their winnings for the next six months. About 2,500 bookies are doing business in Chicago, over 1,000 of whom Capone holds an iron hand, through "the syndicate."

Every night two or three bookmakers are "kidnapped" by squads of Capone's aides and robbed of all the cash they are carrying, while another levy is charged against them, police say. One of the small fry recently was robbed of about $2,000 and told to bring in $2,500 cash and 60 per cent of his winnings for the next six months. "It's for the big shot," he was told, "and there ain't no argument. Kick in, or the next time you go for a ride."

That evening Capone summoned eight of Chicago's top bookmakers to the Hotel Lexington. When they arrived, he instructed all of them that they were to testify

[186]

on his behalf the following day; otherwise they were out of business.

On Thursday, October 15, a columnist noticed actor Edward G. Robinson, "who has given movie characterizations that some believe are Al Capone to the life," present in the courtroom peering at the defendant.

Attorneys Fink and Ahern began the proceedings by referring to Capone's bad luck at the race tracks. Fink pictured Capone as a gambler who hardly ever won. He estimated the increasingly large sums Capone lost year after year as ranging from $12,000 in 1924 to $110,000 in 1929. It seemed that practically all the money the government claimed he made out of his gambling houses, the bookies took away. As Damon Runyon remarked in his dispatch that day:

Your correspondent cheerfully yields the palm he has borne with such distinction lo these many years as the world's worst horse player to Mr. Alphonse Capone.

Milton Held, the first bookmaker, testified: "Al would make bets ranging from $200 to $500 on a race, and he bet on four or five races a day. He usually paid his losses with one-hundred-dollar bills, but sometimes he gave me a five-hundred-dollar bill."

Oscar Gutter, a hunchback who floridly described himself as a "commission broker who handles sporting events, mostly horses," testified that he limited his clientele to "sportsmen who could make big bets; no pikers." Gutter, who kept his derby on until Judge Wilkerson told him to remove it, explained that he considered a person making "a small bet like $500" to be to some extent a piker. Capone's bets always were at least $1,000, Gutter said, and sometimes he would bet $6,000 on a horse—$3,000 to win and $3,000 to place.

Gutter testified that Capone had lost a total of $60,000 on the races in 1927. Asked under cross-examination as to how he tallied the amount, Gutter (who had already affirmed that he did not keep books) replied: "My ledger showed that at the end of the season."

"I thought you didn't keep any books," countered Dwight Green.

"Well, I kept them from month to month so I could pay my income tax." [laughter]

"Why didn't you keep them permanently?"

"Well, it was an illegitimate business."

One by one the other bookies added to the prearranged testimony. Joe Yario, who identified himself as a "gambling broker" operating out of a Chicago speakeasy, referred vaguely to Capone's "two-, three-, ten-thousand-dollar losses," but could not recall a single individual bet.

"Do you know what it is to remember anything?" Judge Wilkerson commented sourly.

Budd Gentry, a Hialeah bookmaker, was questioned by Green as to the names of the horses Capone backed in 1929 for a purported loss of approximately $10,000 each. After a few moments' reflection, he shook his head.

"Can you give the name of just *one* horse that the defendant bet on?"

"I have five or six in mind, but they just won't come out."

Ironically, Capone's elaborate attempt to assemble witnesses had placed his defense attorneys in a delicate trap: taxpayers were able to deduct gambling losses only as they could be deducted from gambling winnings, and both attorneys had already insisted that Capone hardly ever won. In addition, even by accepting the bookmak-

The Trial

ers' testimonies as fact, they accounted for amounts totaling only $200,000. For the additional income, amounting to over $800,000, evidenced by Capone's possessions and expenditures, Fink and Ahern could offer no plausible explanation.

At 3:00 P.M. on October 15, the defense rested its case, having tried to show that Capone was a horse-race addict who lost $327,000 in six years of wagering. It then began making motions, which included a motion for a direct verdict of acquittal; for an order to compel the government to produce certain grand jury testimony and witnesses; for the striking of some of the twenty-three counts against Capone; and for exclusion of a large part of the government's testimony and many of its exhibits. All were denied by the court.

Wilkerson ordered the government to begin its final argument immediately. Each side was allotted four hours, and Wilkerson said he expected to give the case to the jury on Saturday, October 17.

On Friday, October 16, there was a flurry in the court as Beatrice Lillie, star of *The Third Little Show*, which was playing at the Great Northern Theater, joined the spectators with her husband, Lord Peel. Before the trial got under way she had asked to be introduced to Capone, but Capone refused. Later Capone asked who the gentleman with her was. When told it was her husband, Lord Peel, Capone remarked, "Oh, I thought he was a bootlegger."

U.S. Attorney Johnson's two assistants, Jacob Grossman and Samuel Clawson, began the morning session by recapitulating the government's case. Grossman, the elder and more distinguished looking of Johnson's assistants, started off first. Short, somewhat bald, very serious, he spoke in a conversational tone, seldom rais-

[189]

ing his voice. The press had referred to him from the first day as "the logical type, with no sparks." Grossman explained to the jury that what the government was charging was that Capone had an income in excess of $5,000 during the years 1926, 1927, 1928 and 1929 and had paid no income tax. He then proceeded to recount the testimony in a flat, even voice, to show that Capone had enjoyed an income in excess of that sum.

Grossman spoke for forty minutes, neatly reviewing the evidence for the prosecution and the defense. He summed up the evidence for the prosecution:

The government had attempted to prove that Capone once admitted a tax liability and offered to settle on a four-year income of $266,000 [Mattingly's letter]; that he received $80,000 in telegraphic money orders while wintering in Florida; that he owned a gambling house that netted as much as $300,000 a year [based on the ledger and on Shumway's and Reis's testimonies]; and that he spent money lavishly wherever he went.

For the defense, he pointed out that eight bookmakers who had the Capone account from 1924 to 1929 estimated his horse race losses at about $327,000.*

Grossman invited the jury to go with him on a tour which government operatives had taken in tracing Capone's ill-gotten wealth:

"We find him living in Florida like a bejeweled prince in a palatial home. We find that he spent thousands

---

* A statement was made later that day by the Treasury Department in Washington that Capone's lawyers were wrong in thinking race-track losses could be deducted from his income. The Board of Tax Appeals had ruled race-track winnings must be included as a part of a man's income. Track losses, on the other hand, could not be deducted as legitimate losses. If Capone lost consistently, as his attorneys asserted, then the money eventually came from other sources, and he must pay the tax.

of dollars without even thinking twice. We find him receiving thousands of dollars in telegraphic money orders from Chicago. Let's find out how Capone got all this money. He told Florida authorities, trying to get him out of the state, that he was a gambler, a realtor, a cleaner and presser* and a dog race-track owner. He told questioners in Florida that Jake Guzik was his financial secretary. On his income of 'secretary,' Guzik has been convicted of income tax fraud. What about the income of his boss, Capone?"

Grossman reviewed Capone's expenditures—his purchase of suits by the half dozen, $30 shirts by the dozen, $273 bejeweled belt buckles by the score for friends. He added that there was no doubt that Capone owned the wide-open gambling houses of suburban Cicero.

Confronting the point the defense had raised regarding Capone's gambling losses, in which they tried to substantiate the claim that they were "deductions," Grossman set up a neat foil. "Why attempt to prove deductions if we have failed to prove income, as the defense alleges?" he argued.

Grossman then went back to his starting position:

"There can't be the slightest doubt that this man had

---

* The most mercenary of Chicago rackets was the Master Cleaners' and Dyers' Association. It not only skimmed 2 percent from the annual earnings of every member plant, but exacted dues of $220 a year from each retail shop and truck that collected clothing for the plants. It terrorized independents with the exploding suit—a suit sent for cleaning to a defiant plant with inflammable chemicals sewed into its seams. Morris Becker, an independent, defied the Association and filed a complaint with the state's attorney's office. Fifteen officers of the Association were indicted. Clarence Darrow defended them. They were acquitted. Since the law could not protect him, Becker had turned to Capone, who became his legitimate partner. Becker and Capone's Sanitary Cleaning Shops survived and prospered.

a fabulous income, and that he did not want to pay a tax or deal with the government. Finally he was cornered and came in with a special tax man and tried to settle up. Gentlemen, you have the privilege to put the stamp of disapproval on the conduct registered in this case."

With that, U.S. Attorney Johnson's other assistant, Samuel Clawson, took over. Clawson was middle-aged and balding and wore spectacles. He continued where Attorney Grossman had left off, outlining in a precise, calm manner the case against Capone. He pointed out that the defendant knew he was guilty, that he knew he owed taxes to Uncle Sam when in 1930 he gave his income tax lawyer, Lawrence P. Mattingly, power of attorney to represent him to "settle up." Clawson told the jurors that his office had made it plain to Mattingly that while they would listen to Capone's representations, they could not and would not agree that the defendant would be immune from criminal prosecution.

Clawson reminded the jurors of the conference Capone and Mattingly had attended in the office of C. W. Herrick, Chicago Internal Revenue Agent, when Capone was trying to "straighten out" his income tax difficulties:

"Capone was told he could speak or he could remain silent; that if he spoke, what he said might be used against him. . . .

"They were fair to him at this conference. Now, when Capone was asked at the conference if he kept any records of his income, he said no. Asked if he had any property, he said no. He couldn't tell the government what his income was. . . .

"I think it was most significant that Mattingly said at that interview, 'I doubt if Mr. Capone can give you any detailed information on his income.' We will recall that when Capone was asked certain questions on that occasion, he repeatedly replied that he would rather have his lawyer answer."

Clawson insisted that during the conference in Herrick's office, Capone admitted he owed income tax for the years 1926, 1927, 1928 and 1929.

As Clawson spoke, Capone listened intently. A smile crossed his face when Clawson referred to the big bankroll he reportedly carried around with him:

"He always had a roll of one-hundred-dollar and five-hundred-dollar bills—a roll 'big enough to choke an ox,' as one witness testified.* Yet when we tried to get from him an idea of his income, we had no help whatever from him. Why, when we asked him if he went under any name other than Capone, he said, 'Oh, no'; yet in the evidence it developed that he went under the aliases of Ross and Costa."

Clawson scoffed at the idea that Capone lost his income on the horse races:

"One of his witnesses said he lost $110,000 on the races in 1929. He lost all the way from $40,000 to $110,000 with different gamblers. He bought jewelry in vast amounts for his friends. He bought expensive motor cars, and he lived on a lavish scale. Even if he did lose heavily on the races and spent money in other ways, he still had plenty left."

Turning to the defendant, Clawson said:

"Does anybody think that this man did not have a huge income? Why, the idea is ridiculous. Even a child would know better. He had an income that called for his paying to the government a substantial income tax."

Clawson then read to the jury the transcript of Mat-

* H. F. Ryder, the dock builder.

tingly's letter in which Capone, through his attorney, admitted he had a taxable income of $266,000 for the years 1926, 1927, 1928 and 1929.

By noon, it was time for the defense's summation. Attorney Fink rose and faced the jury. He started off by picturing Capone as a modern Robin Hood. "Are they really prosecuting this defendant because of an attempt to defraud the United States on income, or is it just to use that as a means to stow Al Capone away? If the latter, don't you [the jury] be a party to it. You are the only bulwark that can resist oppression in a time of public excitement. Judges cannot do it. The fathers of this country put this power in the hands of the people."

As Fink pleaded for the gangster chief, he waved his arms high, and many in the courtroom, eyes following his gestures, looked to the walls above the jury box. Pictured there was a conclave of the fathers of the country, engaged in making the Constitution.

Fink charged the jury:

"Unless you are certain that Al Capone has been proved guilty exactly as charged in each indictment, you cannot find him guilty at all. The evidence—if it is to be considered as making the defendant guilty—must be clear and convincing and unambiguous and must establish guilt beyond peradventure or a doubt.

"The government lawyers have no confidence in the chaff they have presented here. They know that this evidence of spent money does not prove gross income."

Fink went on to assail the government's contention that Capone had a huge income from gambling establishments in Cicero. He attacked Lou Shumway's testimony, trying to twist it against itself:

"If the figures show Capone made a profit, which

they don't, it does not necessarily prove that he had an income, for he may have been losing money at the same time."

Fink stated that there were two principles involved in deciding the case:

"The questions involved, gentlemen of the jury, are, first, whether or not there is any evidence—whether, in fact, there is any evidence at all that even rises to the dignity of hearsay evidence.

"The second question is the big question, which you are interested in and I am interested in and other generations are interested in, namely: If there be no evidence of guilt, can a jury be persuaded, or 'conned,' into returning a verdict of guilty so that public clamor can be appeased?"

Pointing to the government's lawyers, Fink entreated:

"Don't let yourselves be drawn away from the truth by the claim that Al Capone is a bad man. He may be the worst man who ever lived, but there is not a scintilla of evidence that he willfully attempted to defraud the government out of income tax."

During Fink's argument, the casual Judge Wilkerson left his seat on the bench and quietly paced back and forth at the rear of the courtroom, apparently getting a little exercise. Fink accused the government of trying to prove that Capone owned a Cicero gambling establishment "simply because he was seen in the place. This kind of evidence," Fink declared, "caps the climax."

Taking up the various years involved in the indictment, Fink said the government had no evidence to show that Capone had any income, beyond the fact that he spent money. He scoffed at the idea that because

Capone was said to have named Jake Guzik as his "financial secretary,"* this necessarily meant the defendant had an income.

In a confidential tone, Fink told the jury of a chat he had had with a United States senator, a friend, who was interested in the Capone case. Fink said the senator was surprised when he told him what the government was trying to do to his client. He quoted the unnamed senator as saying: "Fink, you can't be sincere. This can't happen in this day and generation."

Arguing that Capone did not "attempt" to defraud the government as charged, Fink said that if he tried to jump out the window and was stopped, that did not mean he did jump. In other words, the overt act was not committed; it was frustrated. In canonical tones he added: "There must be a 'purpose' or else there is no 'attempt.'"

From the back of the courtroom, Judge Wilkerson broke in on Fink's argument to ask a question:

"Do you think, Mr. Fink, that a man could 'attempt' to defraud the government by remaining silent?"

Fink replied quickly:

"I think that this was the difference I was trying to exhibit to Your Honor yesterday when I tried to explain the difference between 'attempt' and 'intent.' For an attempt to be made, there must be a physical, affirmative act."

Fink ended his appeal on a quiet note. He wrinkled up his nose and gazed fondly at his client, saluting him:

"Capone is the kind of man who never fails a friend. He was loved by his followers. Open-handed, generous, a man

---

* As referred to in the testimony of Joseph A. Brower, Capone's landscaper.

a bookmaker would trust with a ten-thousand-dollar bet. This does not fit in with the government's picture of a miserly effort to evade income tax. A tinhorn or a piker might try to defraud the government, but not Alphonse Capone."

Fink's partner, the elegant Michael Ahern, then rose and took over where Fink left off. W. A. S. Douglas, a columnist for the Baltimore *Sun*, reported:

Ninety percent of the audience were women, a number of whom had to be beaten back almost forcibly from the press seats. They came apparently to hear Chicago's handsomest attorney and most noted present-day pleader. They were rewarded with all the fireworks that go with cases of this sort. Mr. Ahern's voice ran the gamut of human emotions, from the roar of a brave man decrying injustice to the soft notes of a pleader. . . .

Ahern vehemently accused the prosecution of riding beyond the law and of trying to "con" the jury. He insinuated that the government was moved solely by public clamor.

"What evidence have they? Absolutely nothing. . . . The government," cried Ahern, emphasizing his words by blows of his fist on the jury rail, "has sought by inference, by presumption and by circumstantial evidence to prove this defendant guilty. It has sought to free itself from the law, to convict him merely because his name is Alphonse Capone." Ahern then cited an historical analogy. "In Rome during the Punic Wars there lived a senator named Cato. Cato passed upon the morals of the people. He decided what they would wear, what they should drink, and what they should think. Carthage fell twice, but Carthage grew again and was once more powerful. Cato concluded every speech he made in the

Senate by thundering, 'Carthage must be destroyed!' These censors of ours, these persecutors, the newspapers, all say, 'Capone must be destroyed!'"

He warned the jury:

"Be careful of taking liberty from this defendant, Alphonse Capone. You, gentlemen, are the last barrier between the defendant and the encroachment and perversion of the government and the law in this case."

Condemning the government for the large amount of money it was spending in investigating and prosecuting the case, he declaimed:

"By the same token, when the United States Government reaches to all parts of the country for witnesses, spending large sums in this manner, the government is guilty of acts of profligacy. Far better for the government in these hard times to spend this money for soup kitchens!"

Through it all Capone sat with sullen visage, his usual smile missing, moving from his slumped position only to hand notes to one of his two attorneys. Even his clothing was more somber, his tie a quiet color, his shoes a shade less yellow.

At the end of the day's proceedings, U.S. Attorney Johnson announced that he himself would make the government's final plea the following morning and that probably it would take only about an hour. Present in the court was Johnny Torrio. He had been subpoenaed as a witness for the defense, but he had never been called on to testify.

At the beginning of the eleventh day of the trial, George E. Q. Johnson spoke for the first time. He had let his assistants handle the interrogation of witnesses and the presentation of evidence. Now he stood before the jury and addressed them from a sheaf of hand-held notes.

The Trial

From his seat next to Johnson's empty chair, Frank listened:

Gentlemen of the jury, it is my duty to make the final argument of the government in this case. I wish, first of all, to impress upon you the sincerity of the motives in this trial.

You have heard the counsel for the defense state that the government was trying to "con" a verdict of guilty from you gentlemen. Also you have heard him characterize this as a frivolous prosecution.

Gentlemen, the United States Government has no more important laws to enforce than the revenue laws. Thousands upon thousands of persons go to work daily, and all of them who earn more than $1,500 a year must pay income tax.

Johnson paused for a second, then murmured, almost half-humorously:

If the time ever comes when it has to go out and force the collection of taxes, the Army and Navy will disband, courts will be swept aside, civilization will revert to the jungle days when every man was for himself.

Gradually, Johnson traced the early history of Capone, starting with the time when the defendant was a bartender at Coney Island. . . .

He was next heard of at Jim Colosimo's restaurant in Chicago. All this time he was becoming more affluent. . . . Then we come to 1924, when this gambling establishment in Cicero was shown to have a profit of $300,000.

Johnson gestured toward the ledger from the Hawthorne Smoke Shop lying on the evidence table.

Even if we take the defense statement that he had only an 8 percent share, his profits would have been $24,000. Let me remind you that the record shows profits of $215,000 in 1925.

[199]

Then we come to 1926. . . .

Pete Penovich had a little gambling place of his own, which he gave up because of Capone's mob. In the parlance of the gentry, he was "muscled" out. His successor, Mondi, was also muscled out, and after this there was no competition in the gambling business in Cicero.

Johnson then drew attention to Fred Reis's testimony, referring to Reis as a "former associate member of a Cicero gambling resort." Reis, Johnson recounted, "admitted that after taking out running expenses, he bought cashier's checks for Bobby Barton."* Johnson went on:

And Bobby Barton bought money orders transmitting $77,000 to Capone in Florida. Defense counsel was strangely silent about this. Even the mastermind who plans the perfect crime—and this was intended to be the perfect tax crime— slips sometimes.

Capone went to Florida, where he had occasion to spend a lot of money on his house in Palm Island. Again the mastermind slipped when he gave his financial secretary, Jake Guzik, checks to pay his bills.

In a voice growing more heated, Johnson launched his attack on the testimony of the defense witnesses, referring to the bookmakers whom Capone had paraded out on the ninth day of the trial as "so shifty they couldn't look you in the eye."

Johnson repudiated the defense's contention that the prosecution of Capone was prompted by "public clamor":

Can you imagine the federal court considering a case which was the result of clamor? This case has been presented with

* Jake Guzik's chauffeur.

[200]

high purpose and honesty in every step. We have taken great care to get truthful witnesses. It was not a simple case for us.

There is no use denying the great public interest in the case, but we do not ask you to consider that. Treat this defendant as John Brown. Be fair and impartial to the defendant and to the government and do your duty.

As experienced men, look at the whole fabric of the case. You will find in it the design of guilt. Counsel for the defense say this is a case that future generations will remember. I agree with this. They will remember it because it will establish whether a man can so conduct his affairs that he is above the government and above the law. That is what your verdict will write in this case.

At times, as he spoke, Johnson appeared so earnest that he seemed almost evangelical. Clenching his fist, shaking his gray head, clamping his lean jaws together, he dramatically restated the charges. He reminded the jurors that Fink and Ahern had talked to them for four hours, but had "never once referred to the money orders sent from Capone's headquarters in the Lexington Hotel to Capone in Florida." He pictured the Lexington as "the Capital of the Organization," and he recalled to the jurors the testimony* concerning the group of "mysterious men" under assumed names who were quartered at both the Lexington and the Metropole Hotel with Capone.

Pointing at Capone, he exclaimed, "Who is this man who has become such a glamorous figure? He has been called a Robin Hood by his counsel. Robin Hood took from the strong to feed the weak. Did this Robin Hood buy $8,000 worth of belt buckles for the unemployed? Was his $6,000 meat bill in a few weeks for the hungry?

---

* Given by Morrisey Smith, clerk and cashier of the Metropole Hotel, who stated that three or four other men usually occupied the eight-room suite there with Capone.

Did he buy $27 shirts for the shivering men who sleep under Wacker Drive?"

Referring to the vigilante force that raided the Hawthorne Smoke Shop, Johnson went on, "I'll tell you why it was necessary for them [the civic organization] to act, and that's the little notation 'Town'* and $6,000 in the books of that place. That money went to the Chicago town police. That's why the civic organization didn't call in the police. Where were the police when Bragg, that courageous man, was beaten up, his nose broken by the mob outside the place . . . ?"

Johnson warned the jury to remember the men and women who were paying a tax on incomes over $1,500 a year. He contrasted them with Capone, who evaded taxes "during this time of national deficit."

"Let us see how the halo of mystery and romance fits upon the brow of this defendant. Does he ever appear in a reputable business? Did he keep any records, such as an honest citizen keeps? Was there a single instance of contact with reputable business except when he purchased his Florida home?

"Was Capone the little boy out of the second reader who found the pot of gold at the end of the rainbow? If he was not, how did he get the money he spent so lavishly on $12,500 automobiles, $40,000 homes, $27 shirts and $275 diamond-studded belt buckles by the score?"

With head bent, gazing at his listeners, Johnson finally concluded, "The United States Attorney was never more sincere or more determined in the five years that he has been in office than he is in this case in which

* Referring to the page of the ledger included in the illustrations following page 118.

[202]

the facts cry out a violation of the law. This case has been presented with high purpose and honesty in every step."

Finally, it was over. The prosecution and the defense had presented their cases. As Frank Wilson waited for the jury to be instructed, he thought of the long hours it had cost to get this far. Almost three years.

The prosecution's case had been built on the ledger which Frank had discovered that night in the old Post Office Building and which had led him to Lou Shumway and Fred Reis. Mattingly's letter was the final coup. But all of it, although incriminating in Wilson's opinion, could mean something substantially different to a juror. He recalled Defense Attorney Ahern's plea: "What evidence have they? Absolutely nothing. . . . The government has sought by inference, by presumption and by circumstantial evidence to prove this defendant guilty . . . to convict him merely because his name is Alphonse Capone."

It was rhetoric and nonsense, and yet from the beginning that *had* been his task—to investigate and to convict Al Capone. Every moment of his existence during the past two and a half years had been directed toward this goal. And now there was nothing more for him to do.

Before giving his instructions, Judge Wilkerson ordered the doors locked, so that, as he explained, neither he nor the jury would be distracted by the movements of people in and out of the courtroom.

Contrary to general expectation, Wilkerson made no comment on the evidence or analysis of the testimony. He simply informed the jury of the law governing the case. He enumerated the twenty-three counts of the indictments, and after summarizing them he said:

[203]

Now you will see that with reference to the tax for each year, different charges have been made; the charge of evasion has been stated in a different way. With reference to each of these counts, however, the question for you is to arrive at a conclusion as to whether or not the averments of that particular count have been established by the prosecution in this case. When you have done that, you have completed your duty in this case.

He then gave the jury the general rules of law applicable to criminal cases and said that in this particular case the averments in the indictment must be established by a chain of facts or circumstances "strong enough to exclude to a moral certainty every reasonable hypothesis of innocence":

You are the sole judges of the facts of the case. The jury has nothing to do with the question of punishment. That rests with the court. This is a criminal case, and I shall give you some general rules applicable to criminal cases. The indictment is not to be considered evidence of guilt. The defendant is presumed to be innocent until proven guilty beyond a reasonable doubt. He is entitled to the benefit of that presumption.

Judge Wilkerson explained the meaning of reasonable doubt. If the jurors had a reasonable doubt, it was their duty to acquit the defendant. If they believed the evidence proved him guilty beyond a reasonable doubt, they should return a verdict accordingly. In order to convict on circumstantial evidence, the jury must be satisfied that the circumstances alleged were true.

Without using the terms "net worth" and "net expenditure," Wilkerson explained their underlying principles to the jury. Referring to the Mattingly letter, which was the crucial element in the government's case, Wilkerson explained:

The statements of a duly authorized agent may be proof against the principal the same as if he had conducted in person the transaction in which the statements were made. If you find that under the power of attorney and the authority, if any, given at the interview in the revenue agent's office, considered with all the other facts and circumstances shown here in evidence, Mattingly was employed to get together information and to make an estimate and to give his opinion thereof to the Bureau, then the fact that Mattingly made a statement as to what his opinion on that subject was is a fact to be considered by you.

The jury received the case at 2:42 P.M. After the jury retired, Capone hung around the courtroom. Many spectators walked up to him, introduced themselves, and talked with him about his case. After holding this impromptu reception for over an hour, Capone picked up the green overcoat that was the companion piece to his green suit and green hat and left with Attorney Ahern. He remarked jocularly as he walked out of the courtroom: "I don't expect the jury in for two or three days."

That evening Frank had dinner with U.S. Attorney Johnson, his three assistants and Art Madden. Later they were joined by agents Nels Tessem, Jim Sullivan, Bill Hodgins, Clarence Converse and Mike Malone (no longer working under cover). Frank expected any moment to be called back for the verdict. But the hours continued to pass.

Finally, they all returned to George Johnson's office, rather silent now, none of them willing to admit that they were worried. It was like a wake. It seemed unthinkable that they could lose, but there was no telling about the jury.

Frank telephoned Judith. She was crying from sheer nervous exhaustion, but she cheered him on, saying, "Don't worry, you're going to win."

At 11:00 P.M., word came that the jury was filing back in. Frank ran downstairs two steps at a time and fought his way back into the crowded courtroom. When he arrived, Capone was already sitting ashen-faced, waiting. Frank studied the jurors' faces.

"Gentlemen," intoned Judge Wilkerson, "have you reached a verdict?"

"Yes, sir."

"What is your verdict?"

The foreman of the jury handed the bailiff a sheet of paper. The bailiff passed it to the clerk of the court.

The clerk read it aloud.

"Guilty."

The crowd in the courtroom went wild. Reporters ran from the court. Photographers ran. Mobsters ran. Everyone seemed to be running. Everyone except Al Capone.

On October 24, Capone returned to the courtroom and sank heavily into a deep-cushioned chair. He jumped up a moment later, his hands locked behind his back, as Judge Wilkerson began the sentencing.

"It is the judgment of this court that on Count 1 the defendant shall go to the penitentiary for five years, pay a fine of $10,000, and pay the cost of prosecution."

Capone's fingers twisted and turned behind his back. He forced a smile.

On Counts 5 and 9 Wilkerson imposed the same sentence; on Counts 13 and 18, a year each in the county jail, plus the same fines and court costs.

Capone's forced smile faded.

"The sentence on Counts 1 and 5 will run concurrently," Wilkerson continued. "The sentence on Count 13 will run concurrently with numbers 1 and 5, and Count 18 will run consecutively."

It was over in twenty minutes. It added up to a total of eleven years' imprisonment, fines totaling $50,000, and court costs of $30,000—the stiffest penalty ever meted out to a tax evader.

Capone's attorneys, Fink and Ahern, had already filed a writ of appeal with the U.S. Court for the Seventh District, arguing that the indictments had failed to specify sufficiently the means Capone employed to evade income taxes. As soon as Wilkerson had finished speaking, the indefatigable Fink, hoping for a delay, butted in.

FINK: Is it in contemplation that the marshal will take him to Leavenworth now or await the disposition of the writ?

WILKERSON: After I make the order, it is for the marshal to execute it.

FINK: But I think that you might instruct the marshal not to take him to Leavenworth until such time as we have a chance to present our matters to the Circuit Court of Appeals.

WILKERSON: I think he probably would not take him to Leavenworth until Monday in the regular course.

Marshal Henry Laubenheimer broke in: "I am ready to go tonight."

Fink and Ahern stared aghast at Laubenheimer, then turned to Capone.

WILKERSON [to Laubenheimer]: All right. You may prepare the order.

Ahern instantly confronted Wilkerson.

AHERN: Now my understanding of the law is that when we have perfected our appeal, it per se operates as a supersedeas.

WILKERSON: That is not my understanding.

Ahern began citing authorities, precedents that had been upheld in previous cases.

"That does not entitle the defendant to bail," countered Wilkerson. "Under our practice here, I presume the marshal is always to execute the order of the Court unless the Court grants a supersedeas."

AHERN: But Your Honor's order is inconsistent; it is contrary to law.

WILKERSON: I have nothing to add.

As Marshal Henry Laubenheimer handcuffed Capone and led him from the courtroom, an official from the Internal Revenue hurried up with a document attaching Capone's property and that of his wife, Mae, thus preventing them from selling or transferring any assets before satisfying the tax claims. Capone turned crimson. Hurling an obscenity at the tax official, he drew back his foot to kick him.

As he was hauled away, Capone yelled: "I'm not through fighting yet." He was immediately hustled into a special freight elevator. There he found himself next to the man he had known for two years as Mike Lepito. "I'm Special Agent Mike Malone."

Capone shook his head, by this time totally dumbfounded. "The only thing that fooled me was your looks. You look like a wop." Finally he managed a smile. "You took your chances, and I took mine. I lost."

When Capone reached the street, agents from the state's attorney's office, fearful of a rescue attempt, refused to go with him, so Mike Malone and Clarence Converse agreed to guard him.

Outside the courtroom, U.S. Attorney Johnson met with the press. He publicly thanked Judge Wilkerson and the members of the jury, announcing that it was "a victory of an aroused public that demanded justice." Then he added, "It should inspire confidence to know that men like Frank Wilson of the Intelligence Unit, who has been directly in charge of the investigation, should serve the government for small compensation with such great ability and fidelity. . . . I believe this is the beginning of the end of gangs as Chicago has known them for the last ten years."

Frank arrived home that evening by 7:00. Judith was waiting for him. She threw her arms around him. "You did it! I knew you were going to do it all the time!"

Then she sighed, "Now can we go back to Baltimore?"

Frank concluded his investigation in Chicago with a final memo to Elmer Irey:

The splendid cooperation and whole-hearted encouragement of United States Attorney George E. Q. Johnson and his staff during the grand jury investigation and at other times during the preparation of this case served to spur me and the other agents engaged upon the investigations to exert our best efforts to secure evidence and witnesses who could furnish the facts necessary for the indictments. One of the most important factors in the success of the prosecutions was the policy established by Mr. Johnson that all other cases in his office would be subordinated to Capone cases and that the cases should be tried with unusual promptness. . . .

It is also desired to call attention to the fact that as agent in charge of this investigation I received frequent assistance and information of very great value from confidential sources, which was one of the most important factors in the successful conclusion of the case. As the lives of the persons who furnished this information and cooperated with the government during the investigation would probably be placed in jeopardy on account of the vengeance of the Capone organization if their help became known, it is not considered advisable to mention their names in this report.*

Frank then singled out each of the agents involved in the investigation as well as the various assistant prosecuting attorneys.

The *New York Times* editorialized:

Chicago has been terrorized by its gangsters, or rather that part of the population of the city which came closest to them has been. They seemed invincible.

Citing the effect of the Capone trial, the *Times* added:

It has probably made the career of the gangster somewhat less alluring. In that fact, and in the realization that gang rule cannot exist without the connivance or tolerance of great numbers of people who consider themselves law abiding, may lie Chicago's hope.

An event occurring in New Jersey, however, soon threatened to undo the work of Frank and his fellow agents in Chicago. It involved an incident so tragic and so highly publicized that it would arouse the American public to the point of near hysteria. It would also provide Al Capone with the potential means for his release from jail and his return to power.

* The identity of Edward O'Hare was still known only to Frank and to John Rogers of the St. Louis *Post-Dispatch*.

14
THE HEARST SCHEME

In Hopewell, New Jersey, Charles and Anne Lindbergh, with their nineteen-month-old baby, Charles, Jr., had just moved into a partly furnished ten-room house which they intended to make their first permanent home. "Figures and shapes change and vanish in these unsettled times," Milton Mackaye wrote in *Vanity Fair*, "and only the Lindberghs seem eternal."

At 10:21 P.M. on May 21, 1927, Charles A. Lindbergh had been greeted by 25,000 Frenchmen at Le Bourget Field just outside Paris. In the days that followed, all Europe and America read and heard and talked of little else but his triumph. People everywhere seemed to identify with this twenty-five-year-old barnstorming pilot whose solitary flight across the Atlantic had accelerated the world's interest in aviation.

And they wouldn't let him alone.

Such was the pressure put on the young hero that when he was about to wed Anne Morrow, the daughter of the United States ambassador to Mexico, their approaching marriage had to be kept secret until the last few mo-

[211]

ments. "There were no photographs taken," Anne Morrow Lindbergh related. "We escaped in a borrowed car. I seem to remember lying down in the bottom while passing the crowd of reporters at the gate. We changed cars at a friend's house, drove to Long Island, and rowed out to a cabin motorboat left anchored for us near shore. We slipped out into Long Island Sound at night and headed up the coast toward Maine. Two days later we were recognized while refueling at Block Island. For the rest of our honeymoon we were pursued by reporters and photographers in boats and planes. One man in an open boat circled around us in harbor for seven straight hours, his wake rocking us constantly, as he shouted demands that we come out on deck and pose for him."

On the evening of March 1, 1932, Charles and Anne, having finished dinner, sat together on a sofa in their new living room, talking. Lindbergh heard a sudden noise which he later described as sounding "like . . . the top slats of an orange box falling off a chair."

"What is that?" he asked.

Anne had no idea. They resumed their conversation.

An hour later, Charles, Jr.'s nurse, intending to give the child some refreshment, approached the infant's crib in the upstairs bedroom and discovered that it was empty. In panic, she screamed for Lindbergh to come to the room.

Lindbergh hurried upstairs, checked the infant's empty crib, then tore into an adjacent room. Without a word he flung open the door to a closet, from which he seized a Springfield rifle. Confronting his wife, he murmured, "Anne, they've stolen our baby."

By dawn, armies of the press had arrived. City editors prodded their reporters: "There's absolutely no space limit to this story." The general news manager of the United Press declared: "I can't think of any story that would compare with it, unless America should enter a war."

William Randolph Hearst sent the entire staff of his INS photo service in New York to the scene, chartering two ambulances loaded with cameramen and an improvised darkroom in which pictures could be developed.

Hearst had originally met Lindbergh in 1927 when the publisher had joined with MGM in offering the young aviator $500,000 for the right to make a screen story of his life. Hearst was waiting for him in New York when Lindbergh arrived home after his famous flight. But when Hearst handed him the contract, Lindbergh shook his head.

"You know, I said I did not intend to go into moving pictures," he said, referring to an interview he had given to a British daily a short while before.

Hearst tried to persuade him. "This is not a moving picture in the ordinary sense of the word. It is not a fiction story. It is the real story of your life. . . . Do not consider it as a benefit to yourself, but as an inspiration to others."

But Lindbergh was firm. The money-minded Hearst, amazed and impressed by this rejection of a fortune, finally gave him the contract to tear up.

The day the Lindbergh baby was kidnapped, Hearst sent the famed columnist Arthur Brisbane to Hopewell. Brisbane was Hearst's highest-paid editor. In fact, money was so much on his mind that often on meeting people for the first time he would say, "I'm delighted to meet you, sir. Did you know that Hearst paid me $260,000 last year?"

When he arrived at Hopewell, Brisbane ordered New York *Journal* reporter Sidney Boehm to "under no circumstances . . . disturb the Lindbergh family."

Picking up the phone, he then called Lindbergh's private number. "This is Arthur Brisbane. I'd like to come over and talk with you." There was a pause. Then he added, "I don't think you heard me. This is *Arthur Brisbane* speaking." A cloud of amazement came over his face. "Are you sure," he demanded, "that you understood that this is Arthur Brisbane?" There was another pause. Then he slammed down the receiver and turned to Boehm. "You need not take the order about disturbing the Lindberghs too literally," he muttered and stalked out.

Meanwhile, Al Capone had been imprisoned at the Cook County jail. There he continued to preside over organized crime as if he had never been convicted. At one point he was asked by Johnny Torrio to arbitrate a dispute between New York mobsters Lucky Luciano and Dutch Schultz. The Dutchman had been challenging Luciano's claims to certain territorial monopolies, thereby endangering the general peace arrived at in Atlantic City. Capone wanted the Italian and the Jew to reconcile their differences and to work in accord with other gang leaders to reactivate the nationwide organization in which he hoped to play a commanding role upon his eventual release from prison. For the conference with Luciano and Schultz, Warden David Moneypenny permitted Capone to use the death chamber. It amused Capone to preside while sitting in the electric chair.

The Dutchman immediately infuriated Capone by his sweeping demands, carrying on as though the entire New York territory rightfully belonged to him. "If I'd had him outside," Capone remarked later, "I'd have shoved a gun against his guts." What worried Capone even more was that Torrio appeared unaccountably to favor Schultz. The conference broke up with nothing settled.

Shortly thereafter, following anonymous telegrams to the Department of Justice describing the situation at the jail, Capone's privileged life there was put to an end. U.S. Marshal Laubenheimer ordered Warden Moneypenny to ban all visitors except the prisoner's mother, wife, son and lawyers.

On February 27, Capone was playing cards with two fellow inmates when a deputy warden summoned him to the cell door to tell him that the District Court of Appeals had rejected his appeal for a new trial. Capone shrugged, rejoined his companions and finished the card game.

Three days later he learned of the Lindbergh kidnapping. Capone leaped at the opportunity. Immediately he sent word to William Randolph Hearst. With the aid of his "mob," he told him, he would rescue the stolen child.

Hearst, grasping the story's potential, sent Arthur Brisbane to interview Capone. Six days after the kidnapping, Anne Morrow Lindbergh wrote to her sister: "We have come to an understanding with two of the biggest men of the underworld—men who have tremendous power with all gangs, even though they are not in touch with them and responsible for their actions. We do not know where the baby is or who has him, but everyone is convinced it was the work of professionals and therefore can be reached through professionals, and they seem to be convinced that the baby is safe and well cared for. . . . I feel convinced they are sincere and will help us. Isn't it strange, they showed more sincerity in their sympathy than a lot of politicians who've been here."

When Brisbane was admitted to Capone's cell by Marshal Laubenheimer, Capone eagerly told him his plan. He was in a position to do more to recover Charles and Anne Morrow Lindbergh's kidnapped child "than all the detectives in the country."

The next day Capone's plea burst onto the front pages of every Hearst paper in the country, with eight-column headlines screaming:

CAPONE ASKS RELEASE TO HUNT LINDY BABY

Hearst's afternoon dailies carried the same story, with the headline:

"I'LL HUNT BABY IF FREE"

Capone's words were printed in bold-face type:

I'll do anything in my power to get the baby back, and I probably could do as much as anyone alive. I know a lot of people who might be valuable in finding the child. There's nothing I can do here behind these bars, but I'm pretty sure there would be if I could get out. . . .

Brisbane added his own endorsement:

It is possible Alphonse Capone could do that which could not be done by others. . . . It would depend probably on Col. Lindbergh's desire and whether it would be actually in the power of the Judge that sent Capone to prison, or of President Hoover, to make the experiment possible.

Brisbane went on to eulogize Capone's resemblance to a famed Italian condottiere:

Citizens of Chicago interested in Capone's appearance of unusual power should go to the Art Museum on Michigan Boulevard and look at the equestrian statue of Colleoni by Verrocchio, finest equestrian statue in the world. Colleoni had powerful shoulders like Capone's, with a neck and head like his. If Colleoni and Capone had changed places in history, Capone might be riding a bronze horse in Venice today, and Colleoni, who finally left his great fortune to Venice, might be sitting now in the jail on the West Side.

The same article afforded Capone the opportunity to protest his imprisonment:

I handle beer, and beer never did anybody any harm. Everybody is a bootlegger nowadays, either selling it or buying it. The man that buys it violates the law as much as the man that sells it, and has not as good an excuse.

Capone went on to imply that the government, insisting on a share of the bootlegger's profits in the way of income tax, was a lawbreaker as well:

It is as though the government demanded its percentage of a bank burglar's haul.

Regarding his counts of conviction for income tax evasion, Capone remarked,

I don't know where they got those figures, unless it is out of the moon. How do they know anything about my income, since they never proved I ever received a dollar? They may have been able to prove that I spent some money, but that didn't prove I have any income. What I might have had, had been given to me by admiring friends.

This startling piece of promotion by Hearst was carried on the front page of the Hearst papers for the next three days. It resulted in a clamor to free Capone. The clamor grew to such intensity that Anne Morrow Lindbergh wrote to Evangeline Lodge Land Lindbergh:

Mother, by the way, did *not* of course go to Washington to see Hoover about freeing Capone, as all the papers said, but to attend the opening of a library which my father did a lot to get started.

Meanwhile, Connecticut Senator Hiram Bingham announced that it was clear that Capone had "planned" the kidnapping "for this very purpose," to be set free.

Upon hearing of Capone's proposal, Colonel Lindbergh had remarked to reporters, "I wouldn't ask for Capone's release even if it would save a life."

Lindbergh now telephoned Secretary of the Treasury Ogden Mills and asked assistance from agents who were familiar with Capone and his gang. Mills conferred with Elmer Irey.

From the moment the news of the Lindbergh kidnapping broke upon the nation, Judith Wilson had urged her husband to "do something" for the parents of the baby. As strongly as she had opposed and hated the Capone investigation, she wanted him to help Charles and Anne Lindbergh.

Frank had already learned from his underworld sources that Capone had had no hand in the kidnapping; that his entire proposal was a bluff to be freed. After Elmer Irey conferred with Secretary Mills, he telephoned Frank and told him to drive to Hopewell to meet with the Lindberghs.

Leaving Judith in Baltimore, Frank drove alone up to Hopewell. When he arrived he was graciously greeted by the Lindberghs. Later Anne took him on a tour of the house, showing him the spot from which the baby had been removed.

I followed her into the nursery. The crib was gone. All the baby's toys were gone. As she walked toward the window, I saw Mrs. Lindbergh's eye dart for a swift moment to the corner where the crib had stood. Then she set the window just as it had been set the night of March 1st. We walked through an adjoining room. My eyes roved over the walls and I stopped short. Mrs. Lindbergh paused at the door and watched me as I studied the flowered wallpaper. There was something strange about it. I couldn't tell just what it was at first. Then I noticed that on one side of the room the wallpaper had flowers with brightly colored centers; on the remainder of the wallpaper the centers of the flowers were plain.

"Oh, that," said Mrs. Lindbergh. "I've been touching up the centers of the flowers—I haven't finished yet. It's comforting to have something to do."

Charles Lindbergh showed Frank the letter which the kidnapper had left in the nursery when the child was taken. It requested a ransom of $50,000, stipulating that $25,000 be paid in twenty-dollar bills, $15,000 in tens and $10,000 in fives.

"I was impressed with Colonel Lindbergh's simple, direct manner, his deliberate, thoughtful way of speaking," Frank recalled. "In five minutes I felt as though I'd known him five years. Mrs. Lindbergh was a little bit of a thing, terribly distraught, but making a tremendous effort to control herself. She had a dainty, shy quality that I found charming, and her rare, fleeting smile was beautiful."

Frank advised the Lindberghs that Capone's proposal was a bluff. In addition, he told them that he had been assigned to lead the search for their lost child.

Author's Note

Frank Wilson never divulged the identity of his informant within the Capone mob, Eddie O'Hare. Following Capone's imprisonment, O'Hare emerged as one of Chicago's most respected business leaders. In addition to serving as president of Sportsmen's Park race track, he became a developer of legal dog tracks in Illinois, Massachusetts and Florida; he managed the Chicago Cardinals pro football team and added to his wealth through real estate investments and ownership of an insurance company and two advertising agencies.

On November 8, 1939, eight days prior to Al Capone's early release from prison due to symptoms suggesting damage to the nervous system characteristic of advanced syphilis, O'Hare was driving along Chicago's Ogden Avenue when two men in a passing car opened up on him with shotguns. When the shooting stopped, O'Hare was dead. The two men sped away and were never identified.

Years before, John Rogers of the St. Louis *Post-Dispatch* had remarked to Frank about O'Hare, "If

Author's Note

Eddie had ten lives to live, he'd jeopardize every one of them for that boy Butch." Now, with those words echoing clearly in his memory, Frank was determined to repay the man who had so selflessly aided him in his crusade against Capone—and had, indeed, even saved his life.

With Frank Wilson's help, Edward H. "Butch" O'Hare, Jr., received an appointment to the Naval Academy at Annapolis. Emerging as an officer at the beginning of World War II, he trained to become a fighter pilot. On February 20, 1942, he received worldwide fame for singlehandedly gunning down five of nine twin-engine Japanese bombers that were heading for his home base—the aircraft carrier *Lexington.* Flying alone at night in a small Grumman F4F, O'Hare repeatedly attacked the enemy bombers from the rear. As he expended the last of his ammunition, crippling a sixth bomber, his comrades arrived and knocked out all except one enemy formation.

As a result, O'Hare became the first Navy ace of World War II and the first naval aviator to win the Congressional Medal of Honor in Pacific combat. Franklin Delano Roosevelt called his exploit "one of the most daring if not the most daring single action in the history of combat aviation."

O'Hare was promoted two ranks for his exploits and was nominated for a second Medal of Honor before he was killed one year later while pioneering night radar flights near Tarawa.

On September 8, 1949, an estimated 200,000 persons attended the ceremonies in which Chicago's major airport was dedicated in memory of Edward H. "Butch" O'Hare.

[221]

ACKNOWLEDGMENTS

My appreciation to the Intelligence Unit of the Internal Revenue Service, which provided me with their confidential file on the Capone investigation, Case Jacket SI-7085-F.

I attempted to locate the transcript of the trial, *The United States v. Alphonse Capone*, but I was informed by clerks of both the Federal District Court of Illinois and the Appellate Court that they had no record of these proceedings. Finally, a senior member of the Chicago Bar Association put into words what I had begun to suspect: "Looks like Al burned it all." In the end, though, I did locate these records and transcripts, which allowed me to reconstruct the actual trial proceedings. They were obtained through the efforts of Thomas D. Nash, Jr., the son of Al Capone's defense counsel, and I am in his debt.

This book would not have been possible without the help and encouragement of James Byrne, Scott Waffle, Special Agent Dick O'Hanlan, and former Chief of the Intelligence Unit Harry Woolf.

Acknowledgments

I wish to extend my appreciation to Donald Bacon, former Assistant Commissioner of the Intelligence Division; U. E. Baughman, former Chief of the United States Secret Service; Herman Kogan of the Chicago *Sun-Times;* my agent, Henry Morrison, who first saw the potential of this book; and Walter Myers, my editor at Bobbs-Merrill, who guided me, gently helping to strengthen what was there.

I am immensely grateful to my typist, Marge Mila, for her work in preparing the manuscript, and to Louis Grubb and Mary Lamb for their help with the illustrations.

BIBLIOGRAPHY

Allen, Frederick Lewis. *Only Yesterday*. New York: Harper & Brothers, 1957.

Asbury, Herbert. *Gem of the Prairie: An Informal History of the Chicago Underworld*. New York: Alfred A. Knopf, 1940.

Asbury, Herbert. *The Great Illusion: An Informal History of Prohibition*. New York: Doubleday & Company, 1950.

Boettiger, John. *Jake Lingle*. New York: E. P. Dutton & Company, 1931.

Churchill, Allen. *A Pictorial History of American Crime*. New York: Holt, Rinehart & Winston, 1964.

Davis, Kenneth S. *The Hero: Charles A. Lindbergh and the American Dream*. Garden City: Doubleday & Company, 1959.

Dedmon, Emmett. *Fabulous Chicago*. New York: Random House, 1953.

Demaris, Ovid. *Captive City*. New York: Lyle Stuart, 1969.

Bibliography

Ellis, John. *The Social History of the Machine Gun*. New York: Pantheon Books, 1976.

Helmer, William J. *The Gun That Made the Twenties Roar*. New York: Macmillan Company, 1969.

Hynd, Alan. *The Giant Killers*. New York: Robert M. McBride & Company, 1945.

Irey, Elmer L. (as told to William J. Slocum). *The Tax Dodgers*. Garden City: Garden City Publishing Company, 1948.

Koebler, John. *Capone*. New York: G. P. Putnam's Sons, 1971.

Landesco, John. *Organized Crime in Chicago*. Part III of the Illinois Crime Survey. Chicago: University of Chicago Press, 1929.

Lewis, Lloyd, and Smith, Henry Justin. *Chicago: The History of Its Reputation*. New York: Harcourt, Brace & Company, 1929.

Lewis, Sinclair. *Babbitt*. New York: Harcourt, Brace & Company, 1922.

Lindbergh, Anne Morrow. *Hour of Gold, Hour of Lead*. New York: Harcourt, Brace, Jovanovich, 1973.

Lyle, John H. *The Dry and Lawless Years*. Englewood Cliffs, N.J.: Prentice-Hall, 1960.

Lynch, Denis Tilden. *Criminals and Politicians*. New York: Macmillan & Company, 1932.

Ness, Eliot (with Oscar Fraley). *The Untouchables*. New York: Julian Messner, 1957.

Pasley, Fred D. *Al Capone: The Biography of a Self-Made Man*. New York: Ives Washburn, 1930.

Runyon, Damon. *Trials and Other Tribulations*. Philadelphia: J. B. Lippincott Company, 1947.

Bibliography

Sann, Paul, *The Lawless Decade*. New York: Crown Publishers, 1957.

Swanberg, W. *Citizen Hearst*. New York: Charles Scribner's Sons, 1961.

Vanderbilt, Cornelius, Jr. *Farewell to Fifth Avenue*. New York: Simon & Schuster, 1935.

Wendt, Lloyd, and Kogan, Herman. *Big Bill of Chicago*. New York: Bobbs-Merrill Company, 1953.

NEWSPAPERS AND PERIODICALS

The Chicago *Tribune*, The Chicago *Evening American*, The *New York Times*, The New York *Daily News*, The New York *Journal*, The San Francisco *Examiner*, The Miami *Herald*, The *New Republic*, The Baltimore *Sun*, *Time*, *Harper's Monthly Magazine*, *Liberty*, *Retirement Life* and *Literary Digest*.

INDEX

[227]

Index

[228]

Index

[229]

Index

[230]

Index